"Offers tangible help so we can pass on the best of who we are to our children and grandchildren…A tool chest full of help and hope!"

—**Pam Farrel,** coauthor of *Got Teens?*
and *Men Are Like Waffles, Women Are Like Spaghetti*

~

"As the product of a dysfunctional home, and as a wife and mother…I was not disappointed…

"Thanks, Suzie, for the reassuring examples of the healing, love, and sufficiency of our wonderful Lord. Thanks for writing this book for so many women."

—**Kendra Smiley,** conference speaker and author of *Aaron's Way,*
Be the Parent (Moody, 2006), and others

~

"A must-read for mothers desiring to overcome the pain of parenting mistakes they experienced as children…Suzie shows her readers how to rise above the past to leave a legacy of love for their sons and daughters."

—**Grace Fox,** author of *10-Minute Time Outs for Moms*
and *10-Minute Time Outs for Busy Women*

~

"An insightful resource that will bring healing and hope to scores of women. I highly recommend it!"

—**Cheri Fuller,** speaker and bestselling author of
A Busy Woman's Guide to Prayer

~

"Paints a new picture of encouragement, hope, and healing for every mother, regardless of past circumstances…Every woman—every mom—young or old, needs to read this book."

> **—Rebecca Barlow Jordan,** speaker and
> author of *40 Days in God's Presence*

∾

"*The Mom I Want to Be*…encourages readers to grow, dream, grasp possibilities, and savor the moment…A wonderful tool for rediscovering…God's unconditional love."

> **—Jenn Doucette,** author of *The Velveteen Mommy:
> Laughter and Tears from the Toy Box Years*

∾

"Offers the tools you need to break the power of potentially hurtful parenting patterns. Get ready to reinvent your motherhood. This book will set you free."

> **—Caron Loveless,** author (*The Words That Inspired the Dreams*
> and others), speaker, mother of three; www.caronloveless.com

∾

"Eller speaks to readers where they are, and then helps them examine where they have been so they can put their memories in proper perspective and answer the call to a future full of promise."

> **—Kathi Macias,** author and speaker

The Mom
I Want
to Be

T. Suzanne Eller

HARVEST HOUSE PUBLISHERS

EUGENE, OREGON

Cover by Dugan Design Group, Bloomington, Minnesota

Cover photo © BananaStock / Alamy

Back-cover author photo © Larry Watts

T. Suzanne Eller is published in association with the literary agency of Books & Such, 4788 Carissa Avenue, Santa Rosa, CA 95405.

This book is published in association with the literary agency of Alive Communications, Inc., 7680 Goddard Street, Suite #200, Colorado Springs, CO 80920.

THE MOM I WANT TO BE
Copyright © 2006 by T. Suzanne Eller
Published by Harvest House Publishers
Eugene, Oregon 97402
www.harvesthousepublishers.com

Library of Congress Cataloging-in-Publication Data
Eller, T. Suzanne.
  The mom I want to be / T. Suzanne Eller.
    p. cm.
  ISBN 978-0-7369-1755-1 (pbk.)
  Product # 6917551
  1. Motherhood—Psychological aspects. 2. Mothers—Psychology. I. Title.
  HQ759.E428 2006
  248.8'431—dc22   2006001332

Printed in the United States of America

11 12 13 14 15 16 / VP-MS / 10 9 8 7 6 5 4

To the women in my family tree—

my mother, Karen L. Morrison
my sisters, Vicci Gilles and Mindy Stephens
my daughters, Leslie Eller and Melissa Hall

Acknowledgments

This project was an incredible journey, and I want to thank those who took it with me.

I want to thank my mom, Karen Morrison. There were many times on this rocky road when she amazed me with her insight and grace. There were WOW! moments when I realized how much God had healed her, and how beautiful second chances can be.

Thank you, Paul Gossard, for your gentle editing. I felt like I gained a brother on this trip. You were both an editor and a cheerleader. You understood my heart from the beginning, and I'm grateful.

I appreciate Janet K. Grant, my agent. Thank you for continuing to believe in my writing and ministry.

I want to thank Richard. You simply rock as a husband!

Last, I will always be indebted to God. How cool that he believes in us when we don't know how to believe in ourselves.

Contents

Foreword
by Jill Savage

In my 14 years of encouraging moms through the Hearts at Home organization, I've found that most of us became moms before we had any inkling of all that motherhood required. I've also found that few of us ever feel fully confident in the job.

Many women learn their mothering skills from their own mothers. The basic skills of homemaking, relationships, parenting, and marriage are carried from childhood into adulthood. These are the building blocks of a healthy family.

However, not every mom has these basic skills from her family of origin. For some, home was a place of emotional absence. Emptiness. A lack of love. A non-nurturing environment. Nothing was particularly bad at home—there just wasn't much intentionality in parenting.

For others, there was abuse, alcoholism, or other addictions or dysfunctions that destroy hope and self-worth. These moms remember not only emptiness or a lack of love; they may well remember rage, fear, manipulation, or shame also.

Most moms who grow up in a lacking environment vow they will be different from what their parents were. However, conviction carries us only so far. We need something more. The home in which we grew up is where we did our "mothering internship"—now, as adults, as moms, it's very possible we need to do a *new* internship. We need to know what to do with the past, and we need a vision for the future.

That's what this book is all about. It addresses the past and helps moms know how to make peace with it. Most important, however, it shares a vision for the future. It is part of a new internship for moms whose internship was lacking in what they needed as a child…and ultimately as a mom.

Suzie Eller has lived the words in this book. She understands the struggles of which she speaks. She's the real thing—genuine, authentic, and honest. But Suzie is not only compassionate, she's wise. As she has journeyed to become the mother she longed to have, she has learned some valuable principles in the process. What she shares within these pages are the fruits of her personal experience.

If you long for a new internship in motherhood, the book you are holding will most likely be part of that journey for you. Children need a mom who is free from her past. They need a mom who is intentional, nurturing, and full of love and grace.

You are that mom. God has selected you to be the mom your children need. He wants you to find hope, freedom, encouragement, and vision. May you find all of these and more in the pages of this book.

Jill Savage
Mother of five and Executive
Director of Hearts at Home

Looking Forward
to What Can Be

She was fragile and beautiful, with blue eyes and wispy blond hair. I touched her tiny face, amazed—but also afraid. Would I repeat the mistakes of my past? Would my daughter one day carry the same burdens I did as a child? And the most pressing question of all:

How could I be a good mother when I didn't know how?

I'm not alone in asking these questions. One frigid Illinois day I stood behind a podium at the national conference of the Hearts at Home organization. I watched as a diverse mixture of women strolled into the room. Some, I knew, were new mothers with babies. Others were mothers of teens. They came from various ethnic, economic, and age groups. They laughed and talked just like girlfriends, and on the surface none of them appeared to be a good candidate for the workshop I was leading. I struggled with doubt.

Had I made a mistake? Was "Healing the Past" really a good topic for this conference?

The hands on the clock shifted, and whether I was ready or not, this was the moment for me to share. As the fragile thread of my story emerged, everyone in the room fell silent, and we quickly bonded as women with a painful past. Some wrestled with their emotions. Some smiled and wiped away tears. Others leaned forward, attentive—I sensed the connection as I related to their struggles. They were deeper than the challenges of childhood.

They were the baggage we carried into our roles as women, wives, and mothers because of those challenges. We were women who hoped to give our children a different life than the one we'd grown up with.

The class ended, and a line of women waiting to speak with me curled out the door and into the hallway. One by one, they courageously told their stories. Stories of abandonment and of abuse. Some confessed they often doubted themselves as mothers. Many felt they lacked the necessary tools to parent successfully. Their greatest fear was that they might repeat the damaging patterns from their childhood. They wanted to get rid of the bitterness and rage that affected not only their lives, but the lives of their children and spouses. I also sensed hope and determination. These women were eager and excited to discover practical and biblical steps to begin something new. And they were ready to take those steps—so they could push past the past and provide their children with a different legacy.

That Hearts at Home conference confirmed what I've always known.* Outside appearances often mask what lies deep within the heart of a person. Physical or sexual abuse, neglect, and family dysfunction can leave a mark on a person's life.

But so can God.

How do I know that? The once-tiny baby girl I held in my arms is now 24 years old. Leslie is beautiful and she does not bear the mistakes of my past. She is not weighed down with the legacy passed down to me by my mother and her mother before her.

"When we are broken, wholeness can seem either elusive or illusory. Our desperate search for it often takes us on a journey to find that which we have never known," says Erwin McManus, author of *Uprising*. Then, he continues, "when we redirect our energies in this way, we find ourselves

---

* Hearts at Home is "a Christ-centered organization that encourages, educates, and equips women in the profession of motherhood." For more information, see page 221.

giving away even those things we have not received from others. Once we are doing this, the healing process has already begun."[1]

My healing was a journey of faith—trusting God, trusting myself to be the mom I knew I was inside. In my pursuit of wholeness I faced emotions and events I would have rather buried or ignored, but I grew as a woman and therefore as a mother. Along the way I found gifts from God inside of me I didn't even know existed: compassion, forgiveness, gratitude, joy.

I'm thankful you're allowing me to walk with you as you begin your personal journey. Wherever you are in this adventure of healing, I applaud your courage to change the course of your life and that of your child.

I don't pretend to have all the answers, but I will share my story and the truths I've discovered along the way. Rather than try to speak as an expert, I want to connect with you as someone who "gets it." I've experienced dysfunction, and I know how it feels to want to get on with life but still feel trapped. I know what it is to pick up the past over and over again and even to use it punitively. I know what it is to pray and hope for better for my own children and family. And now I know how amazing it feels to lay down the past by offering forgiveness and replacing hurtful memories with brand-new thoughts and direction.

Throughout this book, I will introduce a very courageous woman to you. When I invited my mother to help with this project, she understandably hesitated. I can't imagine how difficult it would be if my children one day displayed my weaknesses or mistakes for the world to see. I'm grateful she consented and allowed me (and you) to peer into her life. Sure, there were times as we worked together that my mother put on the brakes. We stopped and waded through the conflicting emotions that come with digging into the past. Her bravery inspired me.

Something amazing happened as I read the bits and pieces of paper my mother sent to me. My view of her as the mother who was broken when I was a child expanded to include a young girl raised in an alcoholic home.

She became the 15-year-old girl who married an abusive man and bore a daughter while still a child herself. For the first time I realized clearly that my mother was a woman who had desperately wanted to be a good parent, but at one time wasn't sure how.

Just like me. Just like you.

Reading her story helped me understand why things happened in our lives the way they did. More importantly, her life demonstrates for all of us how the cycle of abuse is often repeated for generations.

This book wasn't written to condemn you or anyone else. The journey you are about to take isn't to fix blame on someone, nor is it to label yourself as a victim. Rather, it is a celebration of what can and will be—not only for you, but also for your family.

Will there be a roadblock or two along the way? It's likely. You may get frustrated and angry. You may feel defensive—after all, no one has walked in your experiences but you. From time to time, you might even need a day or two to work through your feelings. All of this is not only acceptable, it's part of the process. If you need to, put the book down for a while and then come back to it.

Just don't give up!

Each chapter, and especially the questions at the end of it, is designed to help you find spiritual and emotional wholeness as you deal with the past. Sometimes discomfort is woven into healing, whether from physical or emotional situations. Here I speak from my own experience as a cancer survivor. When I was diagnosed at age 32, I was given a list of possible side effects of treatment. They were frightening, but the treatment was necessary to rid my body of the disease. In the end, the side effects were worth it because they helped me regain my physical health.

The same applies in this case. As you take an honest look at your past, how it affected you, and how it continues to affect your family today, the process might not be comfortable, but well-being is the beautiful result.

Are you ready? Let's start together right now.

Part One:

Facing Old
Weaknesses

My mother had a two-year-old daughter, but no husband. One day she met a man who had lost his wife in childbirth. He convinced my mother they should get married because he could put a roof over their head and my mom could take care of his child and hers.

They married, and Mom got pregnant right away. Seven months later, my twin brother and I were born premature. I weighed two pounds. I was born without eyelashes or fingernails and had severe respiratory problems.

When I was four years old, my father enlisted in the service after the attack on Pearl Harbor. We moved from Minnesota to California to live on base. My mother was very unhappy, so much so that she packed us up and moved back home a few times. During one move we even stayed in a chicken coop.

Eventually our family moved to a housing addition in San Diego. I was five when a neighbor's grandfather took me to an ice-cream store. He drove me to a grove of trees and molested me. I didn't tell my parents, because he threatened to kill them. But I did tell my sister, and she told my parents. The man was taken to court. I had to describe to the judge what he'd done to me, and he was sent to prison.

When I was 13, my mom still left for a week or two at a time. My father would come home from work and then drive to a little town bar to drown his sorrows. He stayed in the marriage because he loved my mother, but he wasn't a strong man. He didn't know how to pull his family together.

Both of my parents smoked heavily, and I was sick all the time. Because of the discord and the smoking, my home was a hard place to be.

—Karen Lee Morrison, Suzanne's mom

CHAPTER ONE

Shattered Legacies

I pulled my small brown coat tight around me. A sheet of paper crackled on my back.

If you take it off, you'll be in trouble.

I straightened my shoulders and walked across the playground. Little boys and girls pointed at me and laughed. I walked up the sidewalk to the school entrance. It seemed a thousand miles long. When I pulled open the heavy door, warm air brushed my face.

A little boy stopped and stared at me as I passed. I kept my eyes fixed straight ahead and ignored him. I walked toward my class as the bell rang, scuffing my feet against the tile.

"What is this?" A man's voice stopped me in my tracks.

I put my head down. All I could see was the tip of his shoes.

"Nothing."

The principal knelt down and looked me in the eye. He gently turned me around to read the sign tacked to my back with two large safety pins. He stood and wrapped an arm around me protectively.

"Follow me."

His face was dark and angry. I skipped as I struggled to keep up. My heart beat in my chest like a trapped bird. The principal ushered me into his office and closed the door. He knelt and fumbled with the pins, and finally ripped the paper gently away. It felt as if a thousand pounds had been removed from my tiny eight-year-old frame.

The white paper in his hands read, "I'm a Stupid Girl."

"Why are you wearing this?"

My mom had pinned it on me. To this day I don't remember why, but I do remember the scarlet letter telling the whole world I was stupid. I was relieved when I realized Principal Shelstead's face was no longer angry, only sad.

He called his secretary into the room. She paged another classroom, and after a minute my six-year-old sister joined me. He had her turn around.

No note.

I sat beside Mindy, my little sister, on the blond wood chairs. My principal shut the door and called my mother. We sat quietly, stealing glances at one another. Finally Principal Shelstead walked out and told us we could go, and I happily skipped down the hall.

Mr. Shelstead would be in trouble instead of me.

∼

Growing up in the small brick home on Latimer Street involved many contradictions. There were happy times. Some of the weekends we spent at Keystone Lake. My brothers and sisters and I fished with our dad. I swam in the lake. We made lots of noise while Mom read a book at the shore's edge. I explored the woods, looking for arrowheads and pretty rocks. And I loved playing outside with my friends and siblings. We hid in the tree house in my backyard. We explored the playground at Billy Mitchell Elementary. We ran through the sprinkler in the summertime, skipping and running through the spray of water. I was a master at jumping on the pogo stick. I could pogo the entire length of a city block and also jump rope at the same time. All of these are innocent, fun recollections of my childhood.

But those memories are mixed with others that are not so peaceful. I had no choice but to accept the soul-searing punishments like wearing a sign pinned to my coat. I once sat on my front porch with a soiled diaper on my head because I hadn't attended to my baby brother quickly enough. I gagged on pieces of soap scraped across my tongue. I braced for the belt when I heard the phrase, "Line up against the couch and bend over." Many times we all took a belt-whipping if the guilty party didn't confess. I attempted to defend myself when I was whipped with a hairbrush or a hanger. I ran away through the house when things were whipped off the wall to be used in anger. I still hate the giant fork-and-spoon wall decorations that were popular back then!

Life inside the four walls of my house wasn't always abusive, but perhaps that is what made it so difficult. We never knew what to expect. The physical punishments and emotional chaos were inconstant companions. But when I looked at other families, I knew what was happening inside our home wasn't normal.

My heart was gentle, and fighting words twisted my stomach. I hated the curse words and names spoken in anger, and yet I embraced each word as if it were mine to hold. I feared the rage, and yet I fought against it, stirring up additional turmoil.

My mother was broken. My dad paid little attention, burying himself in work or behind a newspaper. Like some windup toy that had been left out in the rain, my mother functioned some times and at other times spun off wildly. I had a beautiful mom, the prettiest of any of the kids in my school. But she was fragile—a stained-glass portrait with cracks running deep through the center of her being.

My mother also struggled with asthma. It is as much a part of her as her brown eyes. Whistle in, soft breath out—a sound I will always associate with her. When I was 13, she started a new regimen of medication. Her breathing eased, but a new dance partner joined the fragile waltz of her existence.

Suicide.

As an adult, I understand that the medication had a rare side effect that produced wild mood swings. But none of us knew that then. It was not only frightening for us, but it would plunge my mother into despair. She disintegrated into huge emotional outbursts over small things. She ran out of the house threatening to kill herself. It was a routine that was all too familiar. While she was gone, we cleaned the house; we did homework; we swept the ugly scene out of our minds like dust out the back door.

She always came back with tears and apologies. She confessed she really didn't mean it, and she would ask for forgiveness. She left tokens on our beds to express her remorse—an all-day sucker was my favorite. But as time passed and new incidences cropped up with greater frequency, it was harder to forgive.

During one of the worst times, her threat of suicide was emphasized with a gun. One day she pushed a gun into her mouth, and I remember I whispered the unthinkable where no one could possibly hear me—"Just do it." I was horrified by the thought, but I meant it. I wanted things to be normal. I wanted the threats to stop. I wanted her to get well because something inside of me was changing.

My mother's brokenness was fracturing me.

Generational Dysfunctions

We can draw lessons from the past, but we cannot live in it.

Lyndon B. Johnson

Dysfunction is often generational, and that is true in my family history. As I dived into my mother's past, I easily drew the connection from my grandmother to my mother to me. Seeing my mother through her past didn't change my childhood memories or erase the events. But it did teach me. There were many benefits gained through this trip into the past. It gave me insight into and compassion for the child who would become my mother. It broadened my perspective— and it helped me understand the "why" behind some of the events and change my own behavior.

It allowed me to ask the most important question: Was I handing the same set of problems to the next generation?

Jennifer Kennedy Dean, author of *When You Hurt and When He Heals,* calls these sets of problems "flesh patterns." They are responses, actions, and parenting patterns ingrained in us by the adults in our lives. Dean says, "Your family has formed your flesh patterns, and you are usually drawn to those who keep engaging them because it's what you know. And even if it gets painful, you probably prefer the familiar to the unknown."[2]

We often parent the way we were taught simply because we don't know better. In my case, pinpointing these generational patterns gave me the opportunity to not only break the cycle, but explore new methods of relating to, disciplining, and encouraging my children. It helped me to view history through the eyes of an adult. I'm no longer the little girl with a sign pinned to my back. I haven't been for a long time. If I want to truly understand what took place and how to change the course for my own children, I have to look beyond my own experiences. I have discovered three truths in this exploration:

1. Dysfunction is often generational.
2. When dysfunctional patterns are revealed, it is an opportunity for change.
3. Understanding the past expands your perspective.

It is human nature to respond to and view life through your own experiences. When you are raised in dysfunction, it is natural to focus on your pain or on the injustices against you. Those feelings make sense because they are your experience. However, your goal is healing—so this part of your journey begins by viewing the dysfunction you encountered through a perspective larger than your own.

You will ask honest questions. What did the offending person in your life experience as a child? What events shaped them as they matured? Why did they bring unhealthy parenting skills or addictions or abuse into your life? As you explore these questions and more, I hope you understand how powerful a tool such knowledge is in this process.

One generational pattern in my family is alcohol addiction. My paternal grandfather was a kind, loving man, but he was also an alcoholic. He used alcohol to escape the unhappy situation at home. My mother's dad died at a young age, but his genetic disposition to alcoholism still lives on in the DNA of our family. Because alcohol is destructive in our family, it is a no-man's zone for me. It is a risk I will not take.

I often listen as women share their experiences of growing up in alcoholic homes. They remember clearly the rage, the out-of-control behavior, and the neglect. Many express anger at the parent who nurtured them less than at their addiction, but it is surprising how many turn to drinking or other ways of numbing themselves to ease their own pain. They do not recognize they are inviting a generational pattern into their own household and into the lives of their children by resorting to a coping mechanism of their past.

Another emotional pattern that emerged in my family history is abandonment. Women in our family fled the scene when things were tough. My grandmother physically abandoned her children for days at a time. My own mother ran from the house or threatened suicide (the ultimate way of checking out of an emotionally overwhelming situation) when life became too big to handle. This is a pattern I could have embraced and passed on.

When I first married my husband, Richard, we had a fight over something trivial. I opened the door to take a drive (abandon the scene). Richard gently stopped me.

"Where are you going?"

"I don't want to fight."

"Let's talk then," he said.

"No." I went into the bedroom and locked the door.

Soon I heard the scratching of a key. My husband stood at the door, a confused look on his face. "Let's talk."

I slipped by him and walked into the living room. For the next 20 minutes we played a game of human chess. I moved from room to room. My husband followed. Finally I sat down on the couch and put my face against the cushions. It seems childish now, but back then, if it was fight or flight, I was going to run, baby, run. So I hid in the cushions, hoping he would just let me disconnect until things were better. Richard wrapped his arms around me gently. My face mashed into the cushions.

Checkmate.

"I can do this all day," he said.

For the next half hour we talked about our disagreement and resolved our conflict. At 21 years old, I had not yet learned the healthy alternative of working through conflict, so I did what was familiar. I adopted the family pattern of abandoning the scene. But I had to learn to deal with the tough times in a way that made me, my husband, and my children feel safe. Fleeing the scene wasn't an option if I was to break the cycle.

Looking at the Patterns

Examining your parents' or guardians' history gives you insight into your parenting skills. Are there destructive behaviors or repeated patterns beginning or ingrained in your relationships? Do you use words that once made you feel ashamed to discipline your child? Do you continually cross the line with your child and then grapple with guilt and regret?

If so, are you willing to start fresh?

The good news is, there are effective ways to deal with emotionally overwhelming situations, such as waiting until the situation is no longer heated, listening to the needs of your child or partner, or compromising to find a solution that will benefit each of you. We'll delve deeper into helpful alternatives later.

The benefit of viewing things from the generational perspective is that it allows you to extend a measure of grace. I never knew the story about my mother being molested at five years of age. This story rocked my world when I read it. As an adult, I was angry that a man had taken a trusting, beautiful child out for ice cream and marked her soul through sexual molestation. Though I may never fully understand why things happened in our home during my own childhood, I do have compassion for that little five-year-old girl who became my mom. It helped me see when her life began to unravel. Refocusing to view her history helped me gain perspective for my own life. David Seamands, author of *Healing for Damaged Emotions,* gives this picture:

> In most of the parks the naturalists can show you a cross section of a great tree they have cut, and they will point out that the rings of the tree reveal the developmental history, year by year. Here's a ring that represents a year when there was a terrible drought. Here are a couple of rings from years when there was too much rain…That's the way it is with us. Just a few thin layers beneath the protective bark—the concealing, protective mask—are the recorded rings of our lives. There are scars of ancient, painful hurts.[3]

I discovered the rings in my mother's life as I came to know her story. I could point to one ring and say, "Here is where my mother felt abandoned," or to another and say, "This is where she lost a child when she was only 18." These rings are the record of her life, and they form part of the pattern of our family tree.

Many of you have experienced sexual abuse, neglect, physical and emotional pain. Perhaps this came about because you were the child of an addict or alcoholic parent. Perhaps your parent is deceased and closure seems out of reach, and you wonder how you can have compassion when there is no opportunity for reconciliation or recompense. Still others of you have parents or guardians trapped in destructive patterns of behavior that continue to affect your life. The thought of allowing compassion into your relationship with them is not only frightening, it doesn't seem to make sense.

Though our circumstances and experiences are diverse, the reason we study the rings of our family tree is so we can discover where drought and excessive rain affected our parents, and therefore learn from it so our children do not experience the same.

Allowing compassion into your mind-set does not mean you condone or accept a parent's behavior. It doesn't mean you don't have a right to be angry at what happened. It simply means that you view the person through adult eyes—so you can learn from the past and grow as a woman and mother.

~

These questions will help you as you begin the process of exploring generational patterns. There are no wrong answers. Take time with each question to look beyond your own experiences and broaden your perspective of the past.

1. Name the parent(s) or guardian(s) who hurt you in the past. What are the rings in their family tree? Were they hurt by others? How did that impact them?

_____

_____

_____

2. Do you see repeated patterns of dysfunction? Name them.

_____

_____

_____

3. With honesty (not condemnation), examine your own life. Are you repeating any of these behaviors or patterns in your relationship with your spouse, your children, or both? Are any of these "flesh patterns" harming you personally?

_____

_____

_____

4. What legacy would you like to leave your children? How is that different from the legacy given to you?

_____

_____

_____

5. Think about this statement: "You can't change the past or the parent(s) who hurt you, but you have every right to grow as a mother and as a person." Are you ready to take that step? How do you feel about the possibility?

_____

_____

_____

_____

Right now you might be experiencing conflicting emotions. That is healthy. It means you are probing deep, taking off the mask so you can be real. That's amazing! But it is also painful, much like removing scar tissue from an old, partly healed wound.

You don't have to do this alone. At some point, when you are comfortable, I hope you will allow God to be a part of the journey if you haven't already done so. Faith was an integral part of finding peace and healing in my life and heart. It wasn't a crutch. Rather, it was understanding that God cares about my journey and me.

You've been courageous today! May I pray with you as you take the next step to pushing past the past?

> Father, I thank you for this beautiful woman. You grieve over the hurts she has carried for far too long, don't you? But you have a plan for her, you love her, and you are delighted in who she is. You accept us when we are broken. You love us when we are searching. You aren't afraid of our doubts and fears and apprehensions—not even our anger. Please wrap your arms around my friend

today so she might feel secure in their shelter. Thank you for her life, for her future, and for her bravery in reaching out for something greater for herself and the next generation.

~

We look inside, and what we see is that anyone united with the Messiah gets a fresh start, is created new. The old life is gone; a new life burgeons! Look at it!

—2 Corinthians 5:17

I watched movies and went swimming at the naval base. I was considered attractive, and the sailors would whistle and make comments. When I was 14, I started dating a sailor. I wanted to hear someone say they loved me, and he did. At 15, I became pregnant, and I married him.

My husband wouldn't let me talk to my family or friends. He kicked me in the stomach when I did something wrong. One day he drove me to Texas to live with his family. His mother didn't want me there because she thought I was flirting with her husband, my father-in-law. When it was time for me to give birth, she drove me to a charity hospital and dropped me off at the door. I was in labor for several hours and eventually gave birth to a girl.

When I was released, my mother-in-law took me to a small, run-down hotel and handed me condensed milk for the baby and some canned goods. Then she drove away. I wrote a letter to my husband, begging him to let me come home. I had no money to take care of my baby or myself. After a month he sent me a train ticket, but as soon as I got back to California the beatings started all over again.

Eighteen months later I had a second daughter. My oldest child was sick, and the doctor diagnosed her with cystic fibrosis. One night I rushed her to the hospital because she couldn't breathe, and she died. When my husband came home, he beat me and kicked me over and over. He said I had murdered our child.

He took the insurance money and drove us to Texas. He would leave for a month at a time, spending money on other women. One day he moved out, and I moved in with a neighbor. After a month, he sent roses, saying he wanted to come back. When he came to the house, he wanted to have sex, but I told him no. He beat me with the roses. He grabbed me by the neck and made me take my clothes off and have sex on the stairwell. I got pregnant that night with our third child.

He left, and I was alone and pregnant. When it was time to have my baby, my water broke. I looked everywhere until I found a coin so I could call someone to help. I walked down an alley to call my girlfriend so she could babysit my daughter and I could go to the hospital.

One hour later I had a nine-pound-thirteen-ounce baby girl I named Tonya Suzanne.

Chapter Two

Broken Mirrors

"I wish you'd never been born."

"I'd date you if you wore a sack over your head."

"You're such a slob."

These were the words I heard at home and school, but they weren't any harsher than those I said to myself: *Stupid. Awkward. Idiot.*

One evening it was dusky dark. Most of the kids in the neighborhood were eating dinner. I sat on the curb with my head in my hands. I had broken Mom's crystal dish. With four siblings, privacy was at a premium and I had stretched the phone cord, which reached from the kitchen to the garage, as far as I could so I could talk with my friend alone. I sat on the dryer in the garage, cozy and content to talk without my little brothers around my feet. I pulled the cord tighter, and it pushed the crystal dish off the table.

My mother was on her way home from work, and I braced for the confrontation. Mom pulled into the driveway, waved, and then went into the house. I had decided it would be better to run away than face her disappointment and anger. I stood up and brushed the dust from my jeans.

Too late.

Mom walked out the door and sat down on the curb. She motioned for me to join her.

"What are you doing out here?"

"I'm leaving."

"Why?"

"Because I broke your dish."

She put her arm around me, a shocked expression on her face. "You think the dish is more important to me than you?"

The truth is, at that time in my life I wasn't sure. It was hard for Mom to work full-time, to have five kids, to take care of a house. I didn't like cleaning near as much as she did. Mom was raised on a naval base, where everything had to be perfect. I thought it was foolish to clean the bathroom sink with a toothbrush every day or to move the couch to vacuum when I had performed the same task the day before. I rebelled because I didn't want to clean for hours after school every day.

I not only felt guilty about the broken dish, but that I had been talking on the phone instead of taking care of the dishes as I'd been instructed.

"Did you hear me? Do you think a bowl is more important to me?"

I nodded my head "yes," tears pressed through my eyelids.

Mom brushed away her own tears. "If you think that dish is more important to me than you, then I'm glad it's broke." She pulled me tight.

At times I struggled with my relationship with my mom, but at that moment I loved her very much.

∽

I heard the phrase "I wish you'd never been born" more than a few times growing up, but I didn't understand everything that was behind it. I didn't get it. I could only ask myself the question, *What was wrong with me?*

I knew that Mom had been married before and that her ex was the father of my older sister and me. But my real dad was Jim Morrison. He had met my mother, now divorced, when she was pregnant with me. Dad was concerned about the beautiful, pregnant young mother living in the garage apartment nearby. He brought her groceries. He played with her three-year-old daughter, Vicci. As my mother's belly grew, the love between Jim and my mom began and grew as well. When I was nine months old they married.

Mom and Dad didn't talk about my biological father while I was growing up. It wasn't a deep, dark secret, but he just wasn't part of our lives. I was close to my father (Jim) and was his child from the beginning. I was only 22 months older than Mindy, my younger sister, and the word "half" did not pertain to my relationship with her or my little brothers Ron and Randy. But I struggled to understand why I felt different when the harsh words came my way. "You are so lazy." "You never do anything right." I was a good kid, and I desperately wanted my mother to recognize that.

To complicate things, I was skinny. Not just thin, but ET-skinny. I appreciate it now, but when I was a teenager I didn't view it as a future asset! Boys who were still gangly beanpoles themselves teased me about my thin body. I learned to put on a front both at school and at home. I acted like words didn't bother me. I learned to come back with a joke, to feign humor at my own expense, or to simply withdraw into my own world. I could hide my pain behind a smile and act as if nothing were wrong. But when I looked into the mirror, the girl staring back at me was a hodgepodge of words that blurred the real person inside.

How You See Yourself...and Where It Comes From

Each to each a looking-glass
Reflects the other that doth pass.

CHARLES HORTON COOLEY

The "looking-glass self" theory was developed by sociologist Charles Horton Cooley, who proposed that people do not form their identity based upon reality, but rather upon how they believe others perceive them.

When a person grows up in a dysfunctional environment and is either actively abused or deprived of proper emotional nurturing, they often adopt a negative self-image. It is a false identity reinforced by words, actions, and circumstances over which they have no control. That person's perception of self may have very little to do with what they see in a looking glass—a mirror.

I didn't learn about the details of my conception until much later, when I was a young adult. It wasn't easy to discover I'd been conceived after a violent sexual encounter, but it did seem to answer a lot of questions. In the beginning, I believed it explained why my mom wished I had never been born. My mother was 20 years old when I was conceived. She had established a peaceful existence after moving away from her husband. Another pregnancy complicated an already harsh situation. She was divorced and made ends meet by cleaning houses. Facing the future as a single mother with not one, but two, children was a challenge. The words "I wish you had never been born" have an entirely different meaning in light of those circumstances.

The truth is, while they were spoken in moments of anger or frustration, my mother didn't mean them. I tacked huge significance onto these words because I was unable to discern the difference between the anger of a fragile woman and reality.

I fought to break out of my insecurities as I moved from childhood to adult life, and I made some strides. But I still struggled inwardly with a lack of self-confidence. I appeared to be shy, but was open with people once I knew them. However, only I knew of the battle that dragged on inside. Trying to feel confident in my own skin was my biggest struggle.

Insecurity can take many forms. It can create an acute desire for control, resulting in perfectionism. It can lead to isolation—trading human interaction for a safer, less challenging environment. A lack of confidence can cause you to build a comic facade that keeps people laughing long enough so you can avoid revealing the depth of your pain. As Erma Bombeck once said, "There is a thin line that separates laughter and pain, comedy and tragedy, humor and hurt."

Finding a New Place from Which to View Yourself

For years I assumed a looking-glass self based upon the words I heard and the chaos I experienced in my home. It kept me from being myself in front of others. It wrapped me in a cocoon of insecurity. But as I started to view myself in a different mirror, I learned four powerful truths:

1. The past is only a small part of who you are.
2. God knows the *real* you.
3. When you grasp your true identity, you don't have to pretend anymore.
4. When you understand your value, you are equipped to show your child his or her worth.

I'm not just a woman who had a chaotic family during my younger years. I'm a mosaic of words. *Wife, mom, daughter, sister.* I'm a woman of faith. I'm a youth mentor. I'm an author and a speaker. I love riding horses on a beautiful Oklahoma day. I'm the first in line to ride go-carts and roller coasters. I laugh until I cry at jokes that no one else thinks are funny. These are bits and pieces of who I am. My past is only one small ingredient. Circumstances, mistakes, words, my childhood, do not comprise my entire identity. They are events and actions and experiences.

This is also true for you. There are many things that make up who you are, and your past is not the chief identifying factor. You discover the real you when you put down your looking-glass self and look fully into the mirror of God's definition of your life. You and I are shaped by our past, but we are not defined by it.

Let's look at my entry into the world.

Was it God's desire that I be conceived in violence? Absolutely not. A man made a selfish choice that marked my mother's life and mine. When I look at my conception through the eyes of our culture, it's not a pretty picture. No one sent out pastel cards announcing my birth. There were no pink and white balloons on the door of the hospital room. My biological dad didn't show up for the big event, nor for the years after.

But this is the good news: My heavenly Father showed up. He was there the moment I was brought into existence, when I was just a tiny cell within my mom's womb. He knew the talents and abilities that he alone as my Creator had placed inside me. He knew I would have a gentle heart. He knew I would have a heart that wanted to write and to help and encourage others.

He knew me—Suzie.

He knows you as well.

The first benefit when you redefine your image is that you stop trying to be something you are not. You unmask and assume the rightful image of who you are and *whose* you are. You drop labels and embrace the knowledge that you mean something to God. You understand that your life is of value. You matter!

As you assume your rightful image, it is as if you begin a fresh canvas. You paint it with truth. It is outlined with positive qualities that are a part of your character. You splash the picture with your hopes and dreams.

Look fully into God's face. Who are you to him? Not your perception, but the truth found in the Bible. These are some of the realities you will find: *You are marvelously made; you are loved for who you are; you were made from nothing into something of value.* Your fresh canvas may not be a masterpiece, but it will be *real.* It shows the flaws you need to work on and allows you to appreciate the strengths and unique traits of your being.

Your True Identity and Your Parenting

As you grasp your true identity, you also strengthen your parenting skills, especially in the area of discipline and encouragement. A mother who struggles with confidence or has a false looking-glass self may personalize the mistakes or misbehavior of a child. *If only I was a better mother, he wouldn't make a C on his report card. If she really loved me, she would clean her room when I ask.* Somehow their actions become less about their behavior and its reasonable consequences than about you.

One of the hardest, and most rewarding, jobs of motherhood is training our children to become self-sufficient young adults. The truth is that children make mistakes. They spill milk on the floor. They throw tantrums in the grocery store because you don't buy them a candy bar. Your teenager might dent the family car, or leave his underwear in the bathroom even after you've asked him to pick it up twice. When you have a healthy self-image, you can separate them from their behavior.

Your children don't understand the events of your past. They weren't there. They aren't responsible for what happened. And, marvelously, they don't understand because you have given them something much greater—a clean slate. I once heard a father remark, "My daughter has no clue what she has. Sometimes I want to take it all away just so she'll appreciate it. Maybe then she would understand what I went through."

The fact that this father's child doesn't understand abuse, abandonment, hunger, constant conflict, or chaos is a gift. He has allowed his daughter the joy of childhood. He can incorporate character qualities in her such as gratitude and compassion. But rather than being based on what he lacked, his experience can provide a series of life lessons as he and his daughter give together or reach out as a family to those with needs.

When your child makes mistakes or childish blunders, he isn't trying to make your life complicated. He is a work in progress. Just like you. You have the opportunity to not only teach him, but form his looking-glass self as you do so. The words you speak are crucial because you have the opportunity to encourage or discourage your child. Does your son realize you believe in him? Does your daughter know what a gift she is to you? (Don't assume he or she knows how you feel. Share it with her. Leave a note on his pillow. Write a note and place it in her lunchbox.) On the other hand, do you use labels? Do you spout angry epithets when you lose your temper? When your son or daughter looks into the mirror of your words and actions, what kind of looking-glass self do they see?

Who is *your* looking-glass self, and how does it affect you and those you love? That's a great question, and the answer you come up with might surprise you. Take a few moments and dig deeper as you look into a different mirror.

1. Describe your looking-glass self (the image you have created based upon the words or actions of others).

_____

_____

_____

_____

2. In light of the above, do you think you have assumed a false identity?

   _____

   _____

   _____

   _____

3. If your past is only one small ingredient of who you are, then describe
   the other ingredients.

   _____

   _____

   _____

   _____

4. Read Psalm 139:13-16 in the Bible. Have you ever stopped to think
   that God sees you as wonderfully made? Do you dare to believe
   that? Does it change the way you view yourself?

   _____

   _____

   _____

   _____

5. This is the hard part, but being honest is key to breaking repeated
   patterns of verbal abuse. Do you ever regret words you speak to

your children? What about unspoken gestures or actions? Based upon your words, what do you think your child's looking-glass self is?

_____

_____

_____

_____

6. What are the changes you wish to embrace today for yourself, for your child, for both? Take a minute and be honest about that. Ask God for help to change.

_____

_____

_____

_____

Let the concepts settle in. Get comfortable with them. You are transforming your thinking. If you need to, let this chapter sit for a couple of days and then come back and study it again. Reflect on your answers. May I pray with you as you work through this chapter?

Father, thanks for making each of us so different, but each with a distinctive plan and design. Help my friend to put down her old looking-glass self today and embrace fully what *you* have to say about who she is. I'm glad she's been honest as she's examined words, actions, and circumstances—both in the past and in the present. Thank you, too, for your affirmation in our lives. Thank you for giving each of us genuine, true words and actions to build our children up as they see and define themselves through our eyes.

&

Oh yes, you shaped me first inside, then out; you formed me in my mother's womb. I thank you, High God—you're breathtaking! Body and soul, I am marvelously made! I worship in adoration—what a creation! You know me inside and out, you know every bone in my body; you know exactly how I was made, bit by bit, how I was sculpted from nothing into something.

—Psalm 139:13-15

I was on my own with my two daughters. I found jobs cleaning houses. I had some assistance to help me feed the girls. You'd think I would be frightened and insecure, but I was actually very happy and peaceful. It was the first time in seven years I could be me. I didn't have to worry about what I said or if I put on lipstick or how I fixed my hair.

When Suzie was a couple of weeks old, my ex-husband came by with a man I had never met before. I didn't let them in because I was afraid of my ex-husband. He said his friend was prepared to testify in court that he had slept with me and that he was the father of my child. I threw a baby bottle at them and slammed the door shut.

About that time my friend Jim came up the walkway to check on us, so my ex-husband and the stranger left. I was angry and scared. I believed he threatened me so I wouldn't ask for child support, so I didn't.

CHAPTER THREE

Becoming Willing to Forgive

I met my biological father for the first time when I was 13. My older sister graduated from high school and sent him an announcement. We were all surprised when he called her. Vicci had left home—she was married at the age of 18 and lived in an apartment. The day he was to arrive, she asked if I wanted to come over and meet him.

I was apprehensive. Any stranger could have walked up to me and said, "Hi, I'm your dad," and I wouldn't have known different. I didn't know what he looked like. I didn't know what to expect.

I was shocked when I saw him. It was the first time I realized that someone looked like me.

My sisters were both blond with green eyes and my mom's small upturned nose. Both were pretty. Ron had light-brown hair with dark eyes and a beautiful face. Randy was blond and handsome.

And then there was me. I couldn't gain weight. My nose was long and slender. My hair was brown, and my eyes were hazel. My arms and legs were so long that my friends at school called me "Stretch."

That's what I noticed first. The man standing in front of me was well over six feet tall. His nose was long and slender. He had hazel eyes and brown hair. He was thin.

I looked like someone. The hazy picture in my mind of my biological father sharpened, and he became a real person for the first time in my life.

~

I met him one more time, when I was 17. I traveled to Texas after I graduated high school and stayed with him and his family. I hoped to ask questions during that visit. Why did he leave my mother and sister alone when my mother was pregnant? Did he know how fragile my mother was because of him? How does a man love three of his children, but not the other two?

I left with none of my questions answered. It wasn't due to his unwillingness to answer them, but because I didn't know how to ask.

There were only two phone calls over the next 20 years, and I initiated both. I stayed in touch with his daughter and learned bits and pieces about his life from her letters. I received a note when he divorced his second wife. I found out that he later remarried, had two more children, and divorced again.

I was nearly 40 when I received the letter saying he had cancer. I sat on the edge of the bed with the note in my hand. Should I call? What would I say?

A lot had happened in the two decades since our last visit. The most impacting was that I had learned the story of my conception. One night my mother let down her guard and shared the details. The knowledge was painful, but by that time my life was blessed, regardless of how I had come into the world. I had my faith. I was married to a kind and godly man. I had three beautiful children. I was speaking full-time to teens and women about how to overcome the past and how to embrace their faith. I was also a cancer survivor. The woman who sat on the edge of the bed with the phone in her hand was no longer looking for answers because she didn't need them. Though there were unspoken, unresolved matters between us, I wanted him to know I cared. I looked at the phone and punched in the numbers.

"Hello?" His voice was fatigued.

"This is Suzie. How are you?"

"Not so great," he replied after an uncomfortable pause.

For the next couple of minutes, I explained that I was a cancer survivor and that I would pray for him. I hoped to encourage him.

"If there is anything I could do to help—" I continued.

The interruption was terse. "Listen, I don't know how to say this. I can't be what you want me to be."

"What do you mean?" I was honestly confused.

"I'm not sure of a lot of things," he said. "For one, I'm not totally sure I'm your father. There are a lot of things you don't know."

I sat stunned as he continued. "I know you are religious, but I didn't ask for you to pray for me. Now is really not a good time to visit." He hesitated, as if waiting for my reply.

I didn't know what to say. The tenuous bonds dissolved into nothingness. I held the phone in my hand for a moment and then whispered goodbye. I didn't understand the conversation or the motivation behind it. The most challenging to comprehend was his choice of last words. His final legacy was the statement, "I don't know if you are mine." I wiped away the tears that slipped down my face. I was a strong woman. The words of a dying man shouldn't have hurt so much, but they did.

He passed away a few weeks later, and I received a phone call asking me to come to his funeral. As we drove to Texas, I fought conflicting emotions. I prayed that he had found peace in the end.

I hoped I would have the grace to say goodbye to something I never really had.

The Foundation of Your Healing

It is very hard to forgive those who have hurt us directly,
especially when they do not feel the slightest twinge of conscience.
If our offender would put on sackcloth and ashes as a show of
repentance, it would be much easier to forgive them.[4]

R.T. KENDALL

Perhaps just the thought of forgiving makes you irate. It is difficult when an offender neither requests forgiveness nor feels that it is necessary. The very act of forgiving goes against our feelings. It denies us the luxury of punishing past deeds. But living a life of forgiveness is vital because otherwise you not only punish those who hurt you, but you penalize your own well-being. Failing to forgive has the power to make you bitter long after the events or people that hurt you are removed from your life. It has the potential to skew your view of humanity, creating distrust of people and their motivations. It traps you in the role of a child long after you are otherwise equipped and prepared to live as a mature and responsible human being.

These were the issues I grappled with as I walked into the funeral home. I could name my biological father's offenses.

I visited with his children and his second wife and met his girlfriend. They were kind. I stopped for a moment by the casket. I was sad I could not fabricate love or grief for the gray-haired man who rested inside. I didn't hate him. I just didn't know him. Two visits in 40 years was not enough time to develop a lasting relationship.

As I walked into the small chapel a man looked up with a surprised expression. Another man stared at me curiously. He stood up and approached me. He introduced himself as a longtime friend of the deceased. "You have to be his daughter," he said. "You look just like him. The resemblance is amazing."

We talked for a moment, and then I slipped into my seat. I glanced toward the front and saw a framed, faded black-and-white picture on the stage. My breath caught in my chest. The young man in the photo looked very much like my own teenaged son.

The service started, and the chaplain read the names of the seven children. Four of them were at the service—the three who were raised by him, and me. My older sister had chosen not to come. His two younger daughters by his final marriage were also not present. I closed my eyes and took a breath, thankful for my husband's presence. Suddenly a scratchy recording of a Frank Sinatra ballad filled the room.

As the lyrics of "I Did It My Way" spoke of having few regrets and doing "what I had to do," I was first shocked, then enraged. Why had I driven hundreds of miles to show respect to a man who had lived *his* way? Why was I at the funeral of a man who had coldly hinted I wasn't his when it was apparent to the rest of the world I was?

I nurtured my anger as I sat there. The "mom" part of me didn't get it. I thought how my children were amazing gifts in my life. I had watched them play when they were babies. I had attended their ball games. I had cuddled with them and read them their favorite stories. I had been in the passenger seat the day each of them climbed behind the wheel of the car for the first time. It was the everyday moments of just being a family I treasured the most. My life was full because of their presence in my life.

Unforgiveness knocked on my heart like an obnoxious, uninvited guest. I wanted to entertain it, make it welcome.

As the service ended, though, I closed the door to those thoughts. Perhaps my biological father had never learned how to properly receive or give love. Maybe abandonment was his defense mechanism when life became complicated. Or maybe he was simply a selfish, arrogant man who lived and died "his way." But no matter what the answers might be, I couldn't change them. I was powerless to turn back the hands of time.

But I had the option to make the next move. Was I prepared to forgive again? The answer was an overwhelming *yes*, because I chose to be healthy emotionally. I refused to pass on a legacy of brokenness, bitterness, or rage to my own family. The cycle had to stop somewhere— and no matter what anyone else chose, I was willing to forgive so I could move forward. I didn't have, or desire, the luxury of doing it "my way."

Later that night I asked new questions as we traveled home: *How many times have my loved ones forgiven me? How great is the forgiveness I receive in my relationship with God? What powerful lessons did my biological father inadvertently teach me about the importance of my physical presence in my children's lives?* Though he had never been there for me, his absence taught me the beauty of what I did have around me every single day.

I leaned back in the seat and watched the stars sparkling in the vast sky and thanked God for the immense blessings in my life. Then I offered up my heart one more time.

Forgiveness is the foundation of your healing. Later, we'll dive much deeper into this subject. We'll discuss how to let go and how to set boundaries if the person continues to exhibit destructive behavior. However, at this point the focus is on you. Forgiveness is a heart issue. It's saying, "I don't want to have these feelings anymore, so I'm willing to consider forgiveness even though I don't feel like it."

When you do this, you start to put down a heavy burden that you've carried for way too long.

1. Write down what you see as the real impact of anger, bitterness, or resentment from the past on you or your immediate family (children, or children and spouse).

_____

_____

_____

_____

2. What are your hopes (or fears) if you do forgive? Be realistic.

_____

_____

_____

_____

3. Take a moment and view yourself as the adult you are now (not the broken child or person of the past). Describe the positive emotional attributes you have to offer (as an adult) to the people in your life: joy, empathy, gentleness, fun, and so on.

_____

_____

_____

_____

4. What if the attributes you've just listed were your legacy to your family (and to yourself)—rather than anger or resentment or bitterness? Would that be a worthwhile benefit of letting go of unforgiveness?

_____

_____

_____

_____

5. Think about the person(s) who hurt you. Remember, you are an adult, not a little girl, and you are not helpless. Repeat this as many times as you need to so it sinks into your soul and becomes truth:

   I'm powerless to change the past. But I have control over how I respond to what happened to me. I refuse to be trapped in the past. I refuse to pass on this legacy to my own children. It is my choice to forgive, to let you go. You will no longer hold a bitter place in my heart. I'm willing to forgive so that I can be free.

6. Share your thoughts about this exercise.

   _____

   _____

   _____

   _____

   ⌇

At this point you can't try to white-knuckle your way through this. Remember, you are not alone. In my case, this is where I needed God the most and where he gave me the strength to be able to push past the feelings of the past. He'll help you as well. May I pray with you as you take this leap of faith?

> Father, you see our willing hearts, don't you? Today we offer our emotions, pain, and our lives to you and ask that you would take that gesture and breathe life into it by the Holy Spirit. We're glad this is your specialty. You take the brokenness of our lives and turn it around. You make the fractured pieces whole. There will be times we'll pick up the brokenness again. Would you please whisper to

us to put it down as many times as it takes, until it's no longer ours to carry? Thank you for a brand-new day and brand-new start for your precious daughters.

~

You're blessed when the tears flow freely.
Joy comes with the morning.

—Luke 6:21

As time went on I fell in love with my friend Jim. We married, and three months later I was pregnant. I gave birth to my fourth daughter, and when she was a year-and-a-half old, we moved to Tulsa, Oklahoma.

Four years later I gave birth to my first boy, and four years later, to another son. Now I had five children. I wanted to be a good mother. When my children were little it was easier. I sewed for them. I kept them clean. I loved them. But when my children were older I realized I didn't have the parenting skills I needed, especially when they were teenagers.

If I had been healed at that time I would have understood that sometimes teenagers just say and do things—and I would have known what to do to respond. I would have known how to be involved with my children in school and sports activities.

But I was sick, and at that time my husband didn't know the right things to say. I knew there was something wrong and that this wasn't the real me. It was why I kept threatening to kill myself. I couldn't handle the horror I was going through or the pain I was causing my children.

Was I equipped to be a mother?

Of course not.

Chapter Four

"It's Hard to Forgive"

"Tell me what I did."

"Mom, how can you not remember?"

"I don't. Not the way you do."

I had an early-morning flight out of Tulsa. I was in the beginning stages of my speaking career, and the airport was close to my parents' home, so I often spent the night with Mom and Dad the night before I was to fly out.

My mother struggles with insomnia, and on the rare times I do stay overnight, we stay up late to talk or to watch a movie. This night was no different. When she brought up the past, I was hesitant. Conversations about my childhood with my parents were guarded. My mother had a totally different perception of the events of the past. On the rare occasions when the subject was broached she pictured our childhood in a favorable light.

Were the memories figments of my imagination? No. I had lived them, but somehow the same moments in history were different for my mom than for my siblings and me.

Mom pressed further. "I need to hear about these things, even if it hurts. Talk to me about it from your perspective."

This was new ground. Normally, this topic was the last thing my mother wanted to discuss, and I wasn't sure the conversation was a good idea. How do you say words like *suicide, physical abuse,* and *emotional abuse* without doing harm? None of them are palatable, no matter how softly they are spoken or how pure the motive.

"It's not who you are now. It's in the past, Mom." I sat down nearby.

"I can't make things better if I don't understand," she replied.

This was a huge step, yet that fact made it no easier. For the next three hours, though, I shared how it felt to grow up in our home. I talked about how frightening it was to have a parent that was suicidal. I told her I felt I had to be the adult and serve as a peacemaker and protector for my little brothers. I told her how the words she said in anger had formed the way I viewed myself. I talked about a few of the punishments that had made me feel small and helpless and angry inside.

There were times it was too much information for her, but she gently nudged me to start again.

I wasn't the only one talking. Mom shared her point of view, too. And through that conversation, I came to terms with the fact that each of us—Mom, me, my siblings—saw our childhood through a different set of eyes. Mom saw it through a haze: being a working mom to five children; struggling with medication that made her feel unstable; battling to overcome the issues of her own past; and feeling she didn't measure up as a parent, especially when we children were teenagers.

Did she remember the bad times? Yes and no. Some of the worst times (and the ones clearest for me and my siblings) were behind a protective wall that blocked out those memories. Mom remembered the feelings and even the threats, but not the actual acts.

"I did that? Are you sure?"

"Yes, Mom, I'm sure."

In the early hours we finally stopped. I felt as if I had buried my fragile mom under a heap of condemnation, though it was she who had pushed the boundaries of the conversation. Mom sat on the floral couch, her eyes closed, her face tear-streaked. She finally opened her eyes and stared at the floor.

"I would change it if I could."

I reached over and hugged her.

We didn't touch often. Quick hugs, but not the sweet embraces I have with my own daughters. Mom pulled me close, and I remained there, resting in her arms—we were two grown women, but also a mom and her daughter.

"Can you forgive me?" she asked.

"I did a long time ago."

That was the truth, but just the fact that she asked was awesome.

Removing Barriers

Never forget the three powerful resources
you always have available to you: love, prayer, and forgiveness.

H. Jackson Brown Jr.

There was a time when I did not want to hear the words "I'm sorry"—when my siblings and I were young adults and the wounds were still raw. We sometimes rehashed the past at family get-togethers. It was a pattern of sharing mutual history, and nothing was said with intentional malice. In private tête-à-têtes, idle comments and perceived actions were dissected:

"Did you hear what she said?"

"I can't believe it."

When stories were shared they appeared to be humorous, but the underlying, even unconscious, motive was to assign guilt. Outside observers wouldn't have understood or caught the implications.

But Mom did.

I appeared to have moved on with my life. I was married, a new mother, but the reality is, I was stuck in a cycle of retaliatory behavior. Long after Mom had moved on in her life, she was locked up in her past because I kept her there. Nothing she did or said could unlock the door. But she wasn't the only prisoner; I was firmly shackled as well.

It was time to forgive. It was neither healthy nor productive to my growth as a young woman, a new mom, or a believer to hang on to unresolved anger. What made this decision difficult was that my mother had forgotten the details. I didn't so much want to make her pay for past actions as I wanted her to acknowledge that they existed.

In *Total Forgiveness*, R.T. Kendall says, "It is my experience that most people we must forgive do not believe they have done anything wrong at all, or if they know that they did something wrong, they believe it was justified." He goes on to say, "Total forgiveness, therefore, must take place in the heart. If I have a genuine heart-experience, I will not be devastated if there is no reconciliation. If those who hurt me don't want to continue a relationship with me, it isn't my problem because I have forgiven them."[5]

Total forgiveness released me from punishing others for the past. It wasn't my job or my right. However, it was my right and responsibility to move forward in my life. My ultimate goal was healing, and I desired to free up the energy I was using to keep unforgiveness alive and use it to pursue greater causes in my life.

As much as we know the benefits of forgiving, it isn't an easy decision. Sometimes it seems impossible, and for valid reasons. Perhaps as we explore six of the reasons it is difficult to forgive, we can remove the barriers.

1. It's hard to forgive because the offense was too great.

When Angela sent me her story, I wasn't sure it was true. Her experience was so grievous that it seemed exaggerated. I contacted her adoptive mother, who confirmed the story and sent copies of a newspaper article.

Angela's story was very real.

Her mother abandoned her when she was seven, but not before burning her little girl's legs on a hot stove. Angela spent three months in the hospital. But when her mother left, her life didn't improve. An uncle and his girlfriend moved in to help care for Angela and her little brother while her dad worked out of town several days each week. The uncle was an alcoholic and came home drunk nightly. He raged at and physically abused the two little children.

After more than two years in this situation, they found relief from the uncle when they moved to Ohio. There, however, Angela's father met a woman on the Internet, and she moved in with them. A year later, Angela—now 11 years old—her brother, and her father moved to Florida to live with the woman's family.

In the new situation, Angela was isolated from her brother. She was abused physically by both her father and his girlfriend's 20-year-old daughter, who banged her head on rocks and tried to drown her in the pool.

Then it was decided that Angela could no longer sleep in the house with the family. She was tied to a lounge chair and made to sleep on the patio. One night, the young girl felt ants crawling over her entire body. She was bitten so badly that her father asked the owner of the house to build a box for her to sleep in. Every night she was forced to climb into the box—just three feet by five feet square—and was covered with a sheet and wire mesh. Then the lid was closed. She breathed through the spaces in the boards to get enough air.

Finally, one of Angela's teachers noticed the scratches, bruises, rope burns, and missing patches of hair. Angela was called into the office— and there she told her story for the first time. The school officials called the police. Angela and her brother were placed in foster care, and her father and others were arrested.

When I got into contact with Angela, who was 17 by then, the amazing aspect of her story was not the horrific abuse—though it was overwhelming—but that this teen had forgiven her offenders. Further, she has been a vocal advocate for abused and neglected children. She has taken the injustices of her life and begun to help others.[6]

This young woman has every reason not to forgive, but she has decided that her father's inability to love and nurture her properly will not deny her the right to love fully.

Did her offenders receive what they deserved? No. They served a minimum sentence for neglect. But whether they are behind prison bars or not, Angela is totally free.

The truth is, you may never receive complete justice for the wrongs committed against you, but living to make another person pay is a bitter and hard road. Forgiving doesn't mean that you invite abuse back into your life, and it doesn't make what happened acceptable. Sometimes it doesn't even make the offenders change their ways. However, forgiving them separates their behavior from your own. It's a full 180-degree turn away from the past. You are not limited by their injustice or by their actions. You have opened your heart to the possibility of greater things than what they chose. They may have left a legacy of pain, but their failure to nurture and parent properly doesn't prohibit you from living a life of compassion and empathy.

I hope to meet Angela in person one day. I want to embrace this courageous young woman who chose to place her wrongdoers into hands bigger than her own so she could go about the business of living and loving.

2. It's hard to forgive because if I do, I'll be hurt again.

How many times do you forgive? As many times as you must to stay spiritually and emotionally healthy. Cynthia Kubetin and James Mallory write,

> We sometimes choose not to forgive because we have a false belief that not forgiving will protect us from being hurt again. Inevitably the opposite occurs. Until we can forgive, we carry the full weight of the offense. The offense continues to affect us as the pain turns into bitterness. Often by refusing to forgive we cause ourselves greater harm than the original offense.[7]

In the Bible, Peter posed a question to Christ. "How many times should I forgive?" he asked.

"Seven times seventy," Christ responded.

Four hundred ninety acts of forgiveness. That seems like a lot, but what do you do when you hit offense number 491? Well, this conversation wasn't about a literal number, but rather a way to live. When you've been wounded, it's tempting to keep record. It's a defense mechanism that says, "Hurt me once, shame on you; hurt me twice, shame on *me*." The danger is that you not only struggle to forgive the injustices of your past, but that you carry this practice of keeping score into your future.

You become an accountant of wrongs, so to speak. This is a type of hypersensitivity that can either make you a very kind and perceptive woman, wife, and mother—or, more likely, it can make you a score-keeper. *Ka-ching—add one more name, one more mark on my scorecard. Add one more reason why I can't let my guard down—because people will do me wrong. They hurt me in the past, and they hurt me now.*

An angry retort from a teenage daughter might just be frustration, but the once-wounded person sees it as a personal affront. A friend may be late for lunch simply because she's terrible at time management, but the once-wounded person doesn't understand why a friend would treat her with such disrespect.

Everything becomes about you. Every slight, every mistake, every conversation somehow boomerangs back to your injured heart. You can't see that if your child is angry and talks back, it doesn't have anything to do with your self-worth as a mother. Rather it is an opportunity to talk with your child to discover the source of conflict or anger, or it's time to apply reasonable consequences for disrespectful behavior.

Or if you're married, for instance, and your spouse doesn't buy you a gift for your anniversary, it doesn't mean he doesn't love you or you aren't worthy of receiving a gift. It's an opportunity to teach a guy who is not very good at buying gifts what you need. He may believe that mowing the lawn and taking care of the family and buying you a hedge trimmer is a proper way to show his love—and may be shocked to discover that you love chocolates and a night out at a restaurant instead of a tidy lawn. What would happen if you stopped chalking up such actions as wrongs and started viewing them as invitations to share your needs? You could transform conflict into contentment as well as learning to offer a measure of grace in relationships.

Let's talk about the people in your past. If they are still abusive or destructive, then there are safeguards you must consider (we'll talk more about this later)—but what if they've changed? What if the resentments you hold on to are ghosts of the past? A forgiving lifestyle allows others to be human. A favorite quote of mine is, "We come to love not by finding a perfect person, but by learning to see an imperfect person perfectly." My mother has grown into an amazing woman, but she isn't perfect. She still tells me I should wear a coat even though I'm a grown woman. And driving with her in heavy traffic is a trip! My husband is an amazing, godly man, but he's not infallible. He gets stressed over finances when I want to trust in faith. My children are beautiful, but we've certainly experienced our challenging moments.

But the truth is, I am far from perfect myself. Each of us must live together, forgiving and giving grace daily, as we call ourselves family. No, you can't afford to be an accountant of wrongs, because it is you who pays the bill in the end—but you can afford to give mercy in your current relationships, and perhaps in those from your past.

3. It's hard to forgive because of the memories.

I was at a Turning Point conference. Because I was working with youth, this seminar taught how to help hurting teenagers more effectively. For the last event of the conference I was in a room with 200 other participants. The lights in the auditorium went out, and a film flickered on the screen. It showed a family in dysfunction. The parents fought and screamed violently. The oldest child shouted back in rebellion. A little boy hid in the hallway and shook in fear. Another child sat nearby, playing as if nothing were wrong so she wouldn't be pulled into the fray.

An older child ran to wrap her arms around her little brother, comforting him. She was clearly the peacemaker, the protector. I closed my eyes, remembering how I used to run into the room and step between the flying belt and my little brothers. I could almost feel the sting of the belt on my back as I screamed, "Stop it!"

I heard someone weeping close by—very close by. Then I noticed tears falling on my hands and was mortified to realize I was the one crying. I stood up and slipped through the darkness out of the room. I ran into a bathroom, into a stall, closed the door, and leaned against the metal wall. I was embarrassed, but nothing stopped the tears.

I heard a knock on the door and looked down to see a pair of red dress shoes. There was another knock.

"I'm sorry, but I'm in here," I said. I reached for toilet paper and wiped my face.

"May I talk to you?" Miss Red Dress Shoes said.

I took a deep breath, cleaned up, and emerged, red-eyed and red-faced. I dabbed a tissue around my eyes. I wanted to slip out quietly to the parking lot and drive away, but the woman with the nice shoes stood in my path.

"Are you all right?"

I lied. "I'm fine," I smiled through the tears and glanced at the mirror. My face was a wreck.

"Can I do anything for you?"

I shook my head. "I'm mostly embarrassed. I don't know why that happened, but thanks for being so concerned." I smiled again and tried to move past her.

"Was your family dysfunctional?"

"Yes." I paused. "But they aren't now. They haven't been for a long time." I took a deep breath. "That's why this doesn't make sense. I'm not here for me. I'm here because I work with youth."

"Which one were you?" She waited, then noted my confused look. "Which child were you—in the film."

"The peacemaker. I watched out for my little brothers. They came into my room at night, and I told them stories when they had nightmares. I took them with me when I went on dates. They lived with me during the summers after I was married. I just always felt like I needed to protect them in some way." I wiped my eyes, wishing the woman would let me go away.

"Why do you think you are crying?"

"I don't know. I haven't ever done this before."

The woman placed her wrinkled hand on mine. "It's good to remember," she said. "It's easy to forget how you once felt. Those memories can help you encourage and help others who are experiencing the same pain."

Those words have surfaced in my mind many times when I've sat across from a hurting teenager. Every time I hear a young woman say, "My family is messed up and no one understands," I ask her to give me a try. What was once painful to me is now healing to the one sitting across from me. They see the wholeness. They know my life and my family. At times, I can almost see their thought process. If someone they respect once struggled with the same thing and emerged as the healed person they now see before them, there is hope for them too.

"We cannot change our memories, but we can change their meaning and the power they have over us," says David Seamands.[8] Your memories can be obstacles, or they can be lifelines to others seeking answers. Your memories can be chains, or they can be keys to changing your response to your own children.

One day I stood outside my daughter's bathroom door. We were both angry. I followed her to her bedroom, where she perched on the edge of the bed.

"We need to talk," I said.

Leslie looked away. I could see how frustrated she was. A guide-line in our home is to not to try to work through conflict in the heat of anger. I was about to break that rule, but then I remembered.

I remembered how I felt when anger or lack of control was the driving force in discipline. I remember how heated arguments would turn into physical altercations. I remembered how helpless and frustrated I felt when I couldn't talk because each word would only spiral into a worse situation.

I hugged Leslie and promised her we would work toward a resolution later that day. Later that night we found a solution without the destructive heat of anger. We were able to hear each other more clearly without the emotion of the moment.

You can hold on to the memories of your past, reliving the events in your mind and heart—or you can remember them for a reason.

In the next chapter, we'll discuss three more reasons it's difficult to forgive. But we've covered a lot of ground. Let's stop for a moment so you can consider the following questions.

1. Do you ever feel like you need to make the people in your past pay for their actions? Name one instance when you tried to do this.

_____

_____

_____

_____

2. What did it provide you in terms of payback? What did it do to the person who was on the receiving end? Was it worth it?

_____

_____

_____

_____

3. "Forgiveness is yours to give or to withhold. No one can extract it from you. No one can keep you from giving it. It's the one thing you have in your power to give as a gift—whether it is received or not." What do you think about that statement?

_____

_____

_____

_____

4. Why is it important for you to forgive even if the person who hurt you has an entirely different perception of the events?

_____

_____

_____

_____

5. Do you ever take things personally that are not intended as a personal affront? Name one instance.

_____

_____

_____

_____

6. Take a moment and consider the conflict you've described above as an invitation to share your needs or to see the needs of your loved one. Put what you (or they) need into words.

_____

_____

_____

_____

The tendency is to beat ourselves up when our weaknesses or frailties are revealed, but I hope you also see your strength in this process. Seeing weaknesses offers the opportunity to change and learn how to do things differently.

> Giant steps, Lord! That's what we're taking as we go under the surface to gain understanding of these feelings. Thank you for making us courageous. Please let us experience your strength, and let us hear your gentle applause as we continue on this journey. Thank you for healing the innermost parts of our being as we give our memories and our families into hands much larger than our own.

I bow my knees to the Father of our Lord Jesus Christ, from whom the whole family in heaven and earth is named, [praying] that He would grant you, according to the riches of His glory, to be strengthened with might through His spirit in the inner man.

—Ephesians 3:14-16 NKJV

One day I ran from the house in a rage. I climbed into my car. I decided I would drive into another car and kill myself. The farther I drove, the more I knew this was something I couldn't do. What if I killed an innocent person? I turned around and drove home.

I had such a big hole in my heart. I didn't know how to forgive those who had hurt me or even how to forgive myself. I was carrying all the bitterness and hang-ups.

When I was a child, I always wished we were a happy family, doing things together. As a child, I don't ever remember feeling like a family. It was always Mom against Dad. My father was my real parent.

We didn't provide our children the things my parents didn't provide me, such as togetherness.

CHAPTER FIVE

A Second Helping of "It's Hard to Forgive"

"Can you name the one person you are angry with?" I asked the teenaged girl.

She twirled a strand of auburn hair between her fingers. "Just one?"

"Okay, more than one. Can you list the people you struggle to forgive?"

She named ten quickly, bending a finger for each one. She would have named more, but I stopped her. "Are these people you are angry with or people you can't forgive?"

"Both."

"Do you love them?"

"I used to. I don't now. Maybe…"

"Do you miss any of them?"

She looked down at the floor. "Not really."

The pain in her eyes said otherwise.

"If you could work on one thing in your life, what would it be?" I asked.

"Maybe I could make the list smaller."

∼

After almost two decades of youth work, I still love hanging out with teenagers. They are brutally honest. They don't wear masks, and they aren't afraid to let you know about their problems as well as the good things happening in their lives.

Unfortunately there is an emerging group of young adults who have no clue how to seek and attain strong, healthy relationships—especially young women. What part does the family play in this trend? Ron Luce, youth evangelist and founder of Teen Mania, says, "Each week in my travels, I see thousands of teens stream forward asking God to help them forgive their parents for the tragic brokenness in which they've been raised. The pain is real."[9]

The next generation needs a model of how to love, how to forgive, how to work through and resolve conflict, and how to stay committed to the people you care about through good and bad times. They are a generation growing up in a culture of broken and fractured relationships. They know how to be intimate physically, yet not emotionally. They seek relationships because they want to connect, but they don't know how to sustain them. They are a generation looking to find healthy role models. And whatever resources we hand our children are what they will present to their children. That's a sobering thought.

The 18-year-old girl I talked with above is a real person. I met her a few years ago after a youth conference. She didn't want anything to do with God (because she was angry with him too), but she did want intimacy. Sadly, she looked to fill that need in the wrong places and with the wrong people. The problem was that once the short-lived physical intimacy was over, she was left standing alone—still with the same heart needs. It was a vicious cycle for an 18-year old girl, not yet a woman, to be in.

I stayed in touch with her for more than a year. Under the tough facade was an angry child. After she dismissed another friend, we re-launched our conversation about forgiveness. Her list of discarded relationships was growing. Aunts and uncles, her parents, her ex–best friends, girls who were "out to get her," as well as numerous young men, all were inscribed neatly in the "out-of-my-life column" in her mind. Even our friendship, though growing, was shaky. Throughout our conversations, she reminded me our relationship was in a lengthy probationary period. I had to prove I was trustworthy. One strike and I was out.

It wasn't difficult to discern that her search for intimacy and her growing list of broken relationships were based on a foundation of distrust. But where does an 18-year-old girl learn how to have such major misgivings about humanity? One comment was revealing. "My mother has always told me I need to watch my back because you never know who might take advantage of you," she once said casually.

A legacy was revealed. Handed down, wrapped in pink, distrust was placed in the heart and mind of this young child by a parent who was loving her the best she knew how. The story behind the story is that the mother had been sexually abused. When the daughter found out about it, she asked her mother if they could talk about it. Her mother brushed her request aside. "It doesn't really matter now," she said. "It happened a long time ago."

This teen lives in a beautiful home. Her parents drive nice cars and work at successful jobs. They take family vacations together. Her material needs are met. In spite of those advantages, she hasn't learned the basics of loving and trusting others. When she views humanity through her mother's eyes, it confirms the warnings, spoken or unspoken: *Watch your back. You never know who might be out to take advantage of you. Pretend your weaknesses don't exist—otherwise people will see them. Trust only yourself.*

Though the mother appears whole on the exterior, the events of her past continue to affect her and those she loves. In a sense, the one who offended her is still abusing her and her family. It is time for this woman to work through the emotions tied to her abuse and restore to health her perception of mankind.

Why are we spending three chapters together on the issue of forgiveness? Because our children need to know how to have healthy relationships. They need to discover how to honor each other and themselves in those relationships. They need to know how to truly heal when they are hurt, so they can still trust. They need to view humanity and the future with optimism. They need relational tools.

They are following our example.

Removing More Barriers

Ours was a storybook home, and our family seemed picture perfect. But as the saying goes, "All that glitters is not gold."[10]

LORI TRICE, IN
ORDINARY WOMEN, EXTRAORDINARY CIRCUMSTANCES

Ralph Waldo Emerson said, "What lies behind us and what lies before us are small matters compared to what lies within us." What lies within you may be untapped until now, but I assure you it is vastly larger than what lies behind you, and it will be with you as you make decisions in the future. What is it? It's the strength that comes from trusting the God who loves you best. It's a gift marked with your name. I hope you will allow God to be your partner as we investigate three more reasons it's difficult to forgive.

4. It's hard to forgive because they never said they were sorry.

Let's face it. There are unrepentant people in the world, maybe even in your family tree. Some people do not apologize because they don't know how. Others do not believe they owe an apology for their behavior. Still others are hardened or enabled by their own destructive or numbing choices. Others offer only what they filter through their own life experiences.

Doug Schmidt, author of *The Prayer of Revenge,* put it this way:

> As hard as it might be to understand, there are people in
> the world who will forever and always be permanently
> remorseless. And if God will not compel them to feel contri-
> tion, certainly we will never be able to do so. While we are
> commanded to offer them the opportunity to repent, the deci-
> sion to acknowledge what they have done must come from
> within. Consequently, we must never allow our emotional
> health, which depends on our ability to forgive someone, to
> remain wholly dependent on that person's willingness to bear
> the burden of what he or she has done—because it very well
> may never, ever happen.[11]

Hurting people hurt people. It's a cliché, but true nonetheless.
However, should another person's inability to say they are sorry keep
you from wholeness? Many women who suffered childhood abuse stay
mired in resentment because they have not received an apology. The
offender's lack of remorse keeps them in an endless waiting game. It
may feel like a position of power for these women, but the game continues on with no end in sight. And there are no winners. (As author Cecil
Murphey notes, "One reason there is so little forgiveness today is that
we, who need to forgive, don't feel forgiven."[12])

Whether those who hurt you are remorseful or whether they apologize is up to them, but you don't have to stay in the game. An apology—
or lack thereof—won't change what is on the inside of you. It doesn't
alter what you can do or who you are. It's awesome if you receive one,
but if you are not willing to forgive before the apology comes, it might
not be enough if and when it does.

My biological father was never able to say he was sorry to me or my
sister, but our emotional happiness doesn't depend upon his apology.
I forgive him. I do so knowing he can never come back from the grave

and make amends. He will never give to us what was never given to him in the first place.

Some weeks after his funeral I discovered the details of my biological father's last moments. A pastor stopped by his room and asked to have a private conversation with him. When the preacher left, his daughter entered her father's room.

Something had changed in him. His face was open and joyful. He was at peace. He pulled his daughters and son close and told them he was sorry for the mistakes he had made—and that he loved them. His son later told me, "If I hadn't known my father so well, I wouldn't have believed it."

Something beautiful happened in his last hour. He accepted mercy from a loving God. He experienced freedom and genuine happiness as he finally embraced who he was supposed to have been all along. Do I wish he had experienced this life-changing moment earlier, when he could have shared it with others? I do. I wish it for him and for his children, and even for my sister and me. But I'm still grateful he found it. And through his example, I learned powerful lessons that have changed my life:

1. Never wait to say you're sorry.
2. Don't delay in accepting what God offers so freely to you.
3. Believe that miracles can happen in your heart and life in spite of the past.
4. It's never, ever too late.

Perhaps one day I will sit and talk with him in heaven. But for now, I'm thankful he found God's grace and love, even if just in time.

5. It's hard to forgive because they won't accept it.

I was opening my gifts at my wedding shower. We oohed and aahed over can openers and blankets and Crock-Pots. I picked up my little brother Ronnie's gift, wrapped with lots of extra tape and love, and pulled out a slinky black gown! I was so surprised I said, "Oh my goodness, I can't believe you gave me this."

My 14-year-old brother had somehow found the courage to walk into a department store and buy a beautiful, long black negligee for his big sister. The look on his face is still etched in my mind. His expression was transformed from expectancy to embarrassment as everyone laughed at my response. I didn't mean to hurt him. I was amazed that my baby brother had bought it and that he had the great taste to pick out such a classy negligee. (I still have it tucked away along with other treasures.) When I think about the courage and love he demonstrated in buying that gift, it still brings tears to my eyes. I didn't receive it properly, but my lack of graciousness didn't make the gift any less valuable.

People may not receive your offer of forgiveness with grace. Forgiveness is not normally a tidy business. You may work up the courage to release the resentment and hurt, and even present your gift wrapped with love and lots of healing tape, but there is still a chance it may be received far differently than you hope.

They may refuse it. They might twist your motives. It may be awkward at best. But even if they turn it away, you still walk away free. What others choose to do with your proposal of forgiveness has nothing to do with what you receive personally by offering it. It's remarkable if it reconciles or repairs your relationship. It's amazing if it starts healing in their life—but if they don't, can't, or won't receive it, that is their choice to make.

Do you see the recurrent theme? Choices! They are powerful. You can't control anyone else's behavior or responses; you are only responsible for your own. The more you grasp this principle, the more you will feel the web tying you to the past slowly unraveling.

6. It's hard to forgive because they'll get away with what they did.

Have you ever thought these types of thoughts?

I'll take a softer line when they've paid for what they did.

If I stay angry long enough, my wrath will make them hurt as much as they hurt me.

They've never learned their lesson, and I won't forgive them until they do.

Your intent is to keep them locked away in an emotional prison until they pay the price. But vows and emotions as deep and anger-filled as these keep *you* locked in as well. "One man cannot hold another man down in the ditch without remaining down in the ditch with him," as Booker T. Washington once said.

One summer day I went to a water park with three friends. We decided to ride down the steep water slide in tandem. We started down, and the swoosh around the first corner felt incredibly swift. On the next turn we slid halfway up the wall, and I screamed as I tried to hang on to my mat. That's when I realized we were in trouble. Our legs were linked, and we couldn't escape from each other. There was a reason riding together was forbidden (something we didn't realize until the ride was over)—the combined weight of four adults made us lethal, like a fully loaded train flying through a tunnel. On the third curve, we flew up the side and then flipped over, landing in an impossible tangle of legs and arms. I slammed upside down and hit my head, only to be thwacked again as my three friends fell on top of me. I saw stars. (Until that moment I thought this happened only in cartoons, but my world was black except for zinging silver streaks and sparkles.) We continued down the slide at full speed in a lump of humanity and landed in five feet of water.

Now I was drowning, tangled and upside down in water. I felt someone grab me by the hair and pull me up, and I sucked in the blessed air. We weren't banned from the park, though we four adults were a poor example before all the astonished eyes of the teens and children who had watched our descent.

I was trapped and committed, no matter how badly I wanted off, because I had locked myself into the human bobsled. In the same way, if you refuse to let go emotionally until another person is punished, you "link with them for the ride." You don't get off until they unlock the gate holding you fast in your seat, and that may never happen. (After all, every day people in our judicial system walk away free even though they've committed crimes. We live in a society and a world that is not always equitable.)

What we are talking about is a years-long pursuit by you of payback, perhaps even after a family member has changed. You hold their arm behind their back waiting for them to cry uncle. You empty yourself emotionally as you engage in a mud-wrestling match. You may feel you are punishing them, but the reality is that you are just stuck in the mud with them.

~

Forgiving is a process, and you not only forgive the big events of the past, but you also learn to forgive a little more every day. Stormie Omartian, author of *The Power of a Praying Woman*, grew up with a mentally unstable mom. She writes,

> As I matured in my faith, I knew I wanted to forgive my mother. I learned, however, that unforgiveness as deeply rooted as mine must be unraveled one layer at a time. Whenever I'd feel any anger, hatred, and unforgiveness toward her, I had to learn to take charge of my will and deliberately pray, "Lord, my desire is to forgive my mother. Help me to forgive her completely." After several years of doing this more often than I can count, I suddenly realized I no longer hated her.[13]

As you become a person who forgives, you discover you can also forgive yourself when you fall short. Instead of living with guilt or condemnation, you see mistakes as opportunities to learn and do better the next time.

You forgive your children and spouse (or ex-spouse). Rather than resenting them or harboring grudges, you work through the problem together and continue to love the person as you find a solution. You forgive friends and co-workers, speaking truthfully about issues that arise, but with tact and love—and with the understanding that you might need forgiveness from them in the future. Living as a forgiver adds a powerful dimension to your character. Many feel that if they forgive, they will lose control or be taken advantage of, but true forgiveness allows you to live life with strength and dignity. Another favorite quote of mine is, "What if the leaders showed up for war and nobody was willing to fight?" Forgiving gives you permission to stop the battle on your part. You won't live a passive life—rather, you will pick and choose your battles.

The same passion you once devoted to nurturing resentment or anger or bitterness will be released for better things. You now have space in your heart and mind to discover the joyful woman inside of you. That's a battle worth fighting!

1. What one thing did you learn in this chapter that you wish to apply today?

_____

_____

_____

_____

2. How much of your emotional energy has been devoted to making an offender pay for their wrongs? To date, what effect has that had upon them? What effect has it had upon you or your loved ones?

_____

_____

_____

_____

3. Where would you like to reinvest that time and energy?

_____

_____

_____

_____

4. Repeat this: "I choose to let the memories come to light. These memories do not have the power to keep me trapped in the past. I will begin writing new stories for my life and for my children." Share a memory you hope you will give your children.

_____

_____

_____

_____

5. Repeat this: "Whether my forgiveness is received or not, I choose to forgive. I choose to be whole. I choose to have a spirit of compassion and strength. I choose forgiveness to be a part of who I am." Write down how that makes you feel.

_____

_____

_____

_____

6. Have you devoted energy to unforgiveness that you are willing to devote to greater passions? Name one thing you would like to invest your time and energy in that will benefit you or your family.

_____

_____

_____

_____

You can choose to regain your dignity and self-worth as you make choices that affect the person staring back at you in the mirror. She's the one who makes the choice to respond with grace. She's the one who will find a new direction in her thought life as she lets go of anger and resentment and fills that place in her heart with compassion and strength.

Something new is happening inside of you. You are not who you were. The old is peeling away to reveal the new underneath it. Perhaps this is your prayer today:

> Father, help me to lay it all aside today. Please help me to live my life as a woman of grace. I'm not big enough to make my offenders pay the price for the wrong things they did. I'm not strong enough to carry this burden anymore. Please give them your mercy in their lives. I won't resist as you change their hearts. But even if they choose not to bend their will or alter their ways, I will-

ingly submit my heart and mind to you. I will walk with you each day as you teach me to how to forgive. I will look forward, not letting the entanglements of the past keep me from what you have for my life.

~

Here's what I want you to do, God helping you: Take your everyday, ordinary life—your sleeping, eating, going-to-work, and walking-around life—and place it before God as an offering. Embracing what God does for you is the best thing you can do for him.

—Romans 12:1

Part Two:

Growing in
New Strength

I was a mess. The medication I was taking had pushed me into severe depression. I was suicidal, and everything seemed black. I was putting my children and husband through a nightmare. I didn't know what was wrong with me. All I knew was that I was scared.

The day I almost decided to run into another car, I came home to find a letter waiting for me on the table. It was from my brother. He was praying for me and felt strongly that I was in trouble.

I called him, and he flew from California to Oklahoma to see me. He prayed for me, and he asked God to heal the hurt from the time I was little until now. He prayed I would be able to forgive all the people in my life who had hurt or disappointed me. He showed me Bible verses where it said God loved me unconditionally, right where I was at that moment in my life.

Until that time I had felt undeserving of anyone's love. I was pregnant as a teenager in a time when it was very wrong to be an unwed mother. I saw myself through those circumstances. I knew I couldn't change the past, but I wished I had grown up before getting married. I wished I had gone to college. I wished I could have achieved all the dreams I knew I was capable of achieving.

But my brother showed me I had something of value. I had my children, and they were gifts to me, not burdens. They were my life, my love, and my heart. When my brother prayed for me, I started to let the guard down in my heart and began the process of healing.

CHAPTER SIX

The Power of Perspective

"Ready, set, hut!"

The football team was on the field warming up for the first game of the season. Cheerleaders waved red-and-white pom-poms and performed a dance. The lights blazed around the stadium. I looked around the crowded bleachers for empty seats.

"Happy Birthday, Suzie!" A teenager from the youth group at church stood and waved. I smiled at her and waved back.

"Happy Birthday!" The wishes were screamed again, this time in unison by several of Melissa's friends. Two girls ran and hugged me tight. Ryan's friend Brandon called me over and gave me a huge hug.

I was 41. I had just rounded the curve into middle age, and it was a nice ride.

As I found my seat at the top of the bleachers, I contemplated the day. Earlier I had sorted through the mail. Among the bills were three birthday cards. I'd laughed out loud at the funny one sent by my brother. I'd checked my phone messages and listened as my mother, one of my sisters, and my other brother had said they were thinking of me on this special day. My mother-in-law had even sung "Happy Birthday." We hadn't had much time to celebrate before the game, but Richard had made me a homemade birthday cake with *lots* of candles. The cards from my children were perched on the coffee table, and a small basket of flowers rested beside them.

The 40s are a decade many women want to avoid. After all, it comes with extras like the beginning of wrinkles, gray hairs poking out of your natural color like antennas, and the dreaded midlife pounds settling in around your midriff. In spite of that, I was happy and deeply content. I wasn't rich or successful. I didn't drive a fancy car. I didn't have the best or biggest things in my house. My skinny days were history, and I had ten silky white hairs hidden among the brown (I'd counted them the day before). But when I'd blown my candles out that day, I hadn't wished for anything because I was already surrounded by so many good things.

~

"You have to be the most unlucky person I've ever met," a friend said one day.

Excuse me?

She laughed at the expression on my face, but quickly sobered. "Think about it. First, you faced hard times as a child. Later, when you had your first child, she had a birth defect and had to have surgery. That caused a lot of doctor bills. Then when you were just 32 years old you found out you had cancer, and you had to go through chemo and radiation." She paused dramatically. "And that meant more doctor bills," she added for emphasis.

I listened.

"Then you and Richard worked really hard to have a farming business, and you had to sell the business and start completely over."

At that point, while my friend took a quick breath, I put up my hand. It didn't faze her.

"Then your son was hit by a drunk driver and was in the hospital for six weeks and had to go through physical therapy and learn how to walk all over again. The drunk driver didn't have insurance—so more doctor bills!"

It was an interesting synopsis of my life.

"Don't you think you've had more than your share of trouble?" she asked. "It's just not fair."

I appreciated what she was saying and was thankful for her concern about my well-being, but I just didn't see it the way she did. Yes, I've faced some hurdles, and some of them can be considered major, but while my friend saw them from her perspective, I saw them from a very different point of view. She saw only the struggles of my childhood. I saw how God had taken someone broken and gently nudged her to wholeness. I saw his healing hand on my life. I looked at the lessons I had learned, such as that adversity can make you strong and that hard times can motivate you to reach out to others as they face the same obstacles.

She saw only that I had had cancer in my early 30s. I knew that cancer had taught me to value life. I learned to never take one day for granted. Battling a serious disease showed me that the things I often fretted about weren't nearly as important as I'd once thought. Cancer showed me exactly what "small stuff" is and what it is not.

The disease also taught me the beauty of birthdays. I can't say I'm so spiritual that I love wrinkles or the extra pounds trying to attach themselves to my waist, but I love getting older. It's what happens in the years that pass that make aging so sweet.

When my daughter and I were planning her wedding, people often remarked casually, "Are you stressed? Are you going to make it through this?"

Are you kidding? Her wedding wasn't a time of stress, but a series of celebrations. When I was diagnosed with cancer, Melissa was eight years old, with soft, wispy blond hair that waved in the wind like a dandelion gone to seed. She cuddled with me in my hospital room after surgery. She walked in to sleep beside me after chemotherapy with her Care Bear sleeping bag wrapped around her little body. She laid her small hands on me and prayed that her momma would survive. So going to wedding shows with her, helping her pick between tulle and satin, choosing a cake—and sitting on the front row as my beautiful girl, all grown up, walked down the aisle—was a gift of great magnitude.

Perspective!

My friend's point of view was that an irresponsible drunk had hurt my son and it wasn't fair to our family. This is perhaps closest to the truth. It is the hardest event to view in a positive light because when Ryan was hurt, it was harder than cancer and more difficult than financial hardships. There is something inside of every mom that wants to protect her child. It's the part of us that springs into action when a child steps off the curb without looking or when someone callously harms our little (or big) son or daughter.

My son was 15 when he was injured in the wreck. A drunk driver passed out behind the wheel and crashed into Ryan and his two friends. All Ryan remembers is bright lights flashing, his friend screaming, and the engine of the truck pushing into the cab as the car crashed into them at 70 miles per hour.

The wreck stole Ryan's dreams of excelling in track and basketball. The first few weeks at the hospital left us fatigued and overwhelmed. The drunk driver died on impact, and he was underinsured. The hospital stay and a year of physical therapy were expensive and time-consuming, and doctor bills stacked up, one on top of another. I wrestled with anger over the dead man's choice, but also with grief that he'd lost his life.

But even that time of our lives contained good things. Friends and family brought food, and they mowed our yard and cleaned our house. They decorated Ryan's hospital room with pictures and handmade posters. They brought him special treats and sat with him while we ran home to shower and change clothes.

One night, though, I was fatigued physically and emotionally. Ryan was in traction because of 13 fractures from the waist down. He was in severe pain, and the medication wasn't helping. Richard came to the hospital after work and gently forced me to take a break. Instead of going to the cafeteria, I found a small empty waiting room. I slid down the wall, rested my head on my knees, and started crying.

My son was broken, and I didn't know how to fix him.

A friend from church walked by and saw me sitting on the floor. She sat down in front of me, and she picked up my foot and began to gently rub it. She didn't know the right words to say, but her compassionate act was beautiful. Her gesture felt like the hands of Christ massaging my feet. It was as if he were in that sterile waiting room right beside me, saying, "I'm with you, Sis. I'll help you through this. You are not alone."

Yes, it was a dark time, but it was also a time where I felt God through the love and compassion of friends and family and our community. I saw my son's spiritual maturity increase as he trusted God with a youthful, strong faith.

Perspective is powerful. It can be a set of dark glasses through which we view life, others, and even ourselves. Or it can be a brightly lit window through which we learn lessons from the harder moments and events—and recognize those who support us during those difficult times.

If I choose to look at the dark times only, I'm afraid I'll miss the light. It's not that I deny the tough stuff, but when I turn away from the past long enough to count the good things around me, I can't help but acknowledge what I've been given.

That's what I saw the day I walked up the bleachers to find my seat. I knew 40 was now a reality and 50 was just around the corner. But what stands out about that day are the small things—handwritten notes on birthday cards, teenagers who stood up in the stands to scream out Happy Birthday, a cake made from a mix, a basket of yellow mums.

Little things, but also priceless gifts.

Sources of Perspective

*There are only two ways to live your life. One is as if
nothing is a miracle. The other is as though everything is a miracle.*

ALBERT EINSTEIN

If you desire to study diverse temperaments, I invite you to visit
the Eller house at 6 AM. My husband and oldest daughter wake up
with a smile. (When Leslie visits from college, I love waking her up.
Her first words are, "I love you.") Richard whistles and sings, even at
5:30 AM when he is getting ready for work. It's not unusual to hear me
request, "Please, sweetheart, no singing before 7 AM." If I am awake I
walk around the house quietly with little enthusiasm. I'm not cranky—
I'm basically still in the sleep mode.

Temperament goes beyond night owls versus morning people. Some
of you are optimistic, others pessimistic. Some are slow to get angry,
while others of you struggle with your temper. Some of you are naturally
merciful, while others are not. It's the basic foundation of our personality, and the way we arrived in the world.

You build upon that foundation as you encounter life experiences,
whether positive or negative. As a youth worker, I meet 13-year-old
girls who are still innocent, still in that gap between child and teen. I
also work with 13-year-old girls who are already making destructive life
choices and who are critical of life and authority. Ninety-nine percent
of the time the difference is their life experiences.

Your background or environment also affects your perspective. My
husband, Richard, was raised on a dairy farm. I was raised in the city.
When we met, he knew where milk came from. So did I—it came from
the grocery store, of course!

That was only one of our clashes of perspective. Our diverse back-
grounds created some hilarious moments. When we were dating, he
gave me directions to a friend's house, where I was to pick him up. His

friend lived in a small community in Oklahoma. Richard told me to take the highway, turn off at a certain exit, and then take several dirt roads. One of the instructions was to turn right at the Y in the road. I was doing great until then. I searched, but I finally gave up because I could not find the Y. I drove back to town and made a phone call. Richard burst into laughter when I said, "I've been looking for a YMCA everywhere, and there just isn't one."

A "Y" in the road held very different meanings for the city girl and the country guy.

The dilemma comes when we allow ourselves to be limited by the factors that form our perception. It's easy to point to your temperament and say to others, "That's just the way I am—deal with it." I could use this excuse and fire away at my family in the early hours of the day because my natural disposition is not to be a morning person. However, the theory that you are stuck with what you've been given shoots down the idea of personal growth. Life circumstances become an excuse for a negative approach to life, marriage, and to parenting.

Shifting Your Perspective

One way to change your perspective is to begin to examine what Paul Harvey calls "the rest of the story." In the Bible, a widow named Naomi was bitter over her loss of her husband and sons, and her outlook on life was gloomy. She left her home to find a new place to live. Her two daughters-in-law followed and she indicated she wanted them to leave her alone. All she wanted was to continue on her solitary journey. One daughter-in-law listened and turned back, but the other, Ruth, clung to her and refused to leave her.

They traveled on together as companions. Later, they met a distant relative named Boaz. This man probably recognized that Naomi was bitter. His generous actions toward Ruth, her daughter-in-law, challenged Naomi to look past her losses to see the good things. Boaz shifted her perspective from her grief to the faithful daughter-in-law who had left everything behind to be a friend.[15]

Until that time, it seems Naomi could see only her sadness. She was insensitive to the fact that not only she had lost loved ones. Ruth had lost her husband. Broadening her perspective didn't minimize the death of Naomi's family members, but it did allow her to see beyond her losses. It was at that point she could begin to heal.

What are your miracles? Have you stopped to count them lately? Do you appreciate the beauty all around you? Do you see your daughter's smile? Can you describe the touch of a baby's finger on your cheek? Have you stopped long enough to smell honeysuckle on a warm summer day? If you're married, do you appreciate your husband's laugh? Have you noticed the grandeur of stars on a clear night?

What about the smaller things? The taste of ice cream with caramel and whipped cream. Conversations with good friends. The handwritten notes from your grade-school-aged child. There are small and large gifts awaiting to be opened and appreciated every single day.

In 2005, during the time I was writing this book, Hurricane Katrina wiped out an entire city. Several thousand evacuees from New Orleans were bused to a military camp near us. Though these people had experienced horrendous loss, it was the small things they appreciated: clean clothes, a toothbrush, a pillow. One woman, after spending her first week in northeastern Oklahoma, said, "I love it here. I love the green grass and the open sky. I love the people who are so kind." She had lost everything, but suddenly it was the everyday things often taken for granted that seemed to be the most exquisite. Observing this disaster confirmed to me four principles about perspective:

1. We don't know what we have until we lose it.

2. When all is said and done, it is the things we take most for granted that are the most enduring.

3. Life will continue to present us with good things and

difficult things. Within every life circumstance and event lies a moment in which we can learn and grow.

4. Our perspective is not limited by temperament, circumstances, or other people.

Allowing our perception to expand is one of the most powerful tools we have to unlock the mysteries of joy. Ernest Hemingway said, "Never write about a place until you're away from it, because that gives you perspective." Perhaps he is saying that many people and places and things are seen with their real value when we can no longer take them for granted.

You have within you the potential to continue to grow, to dream, to grasp the possibilities, and to savor the moments. When you do this, you begin to glimpse the many miracles of life—through the power of perspective.

Author and speaker Robert Bly says, "When a father, absent during the day, returns home at six, his children receive only his temperament, not his teaching." As you answer the following questions, think about how your perspective—your temperament, your outlook and response to life—affect your family. Is it positive? Is it balanced? Does it point to the past and fail to look at the present?

1. Do you ever use the excuse "That's just the way I am"?

_____

_____

_____

_____

2. What are the temperaments of others in your family? Describe each.

_____

_____

_____

_____

3. Does your perspective on your past affect your family today? In what ways?

_____

_____

_____

_____

4. Name five good things in your life.

_____

_____

_____

_____

5. What does it mean to you to have a balanced perspective?

_____

_____

_____

_____

6. Earlier you named five good things in your life. Now go beyond the obvious. What are ten smaller, ordinary good things (favorite food, smells, sights) you would miss if they were taken away?

_____

_____

_____

_____

7. Life's circumstances have shaped you. Name a positive attribute or attitude that has come out of those difficulties.

_____

_____

_____

_____

8. Was there one thought that stood out to you as you read this chapter on perspective? What was it, and how does it personally relate to you or your family?

_____

_____

_____

_____

I read several books each week, and one recent morning I read a passage that challenged me. It made me rethink the way I thought about what I do for people and how I serve them. In the words of this author, an ordinary man, God showed me a small spark of truth that ignited in me a brand-new way to perceive what I was doing. Perhaps you have also had a few of those moments. They may not trigger change overnight, but every great event or occurrence begins as a thought. Small things produce a ripple effect that continues to move you toward deeper waters. You may find yourself saying, *Maybe this can happen in my life. Maybe this is something I could try.*

You won't wake up tomorrow with a completely altered perspective, but you will have started something new. You might look at your child's sleeping face and, despite your fatigue, sense the greatness of this little person in your life. You might find yourself refocusing—balancing your past with the good things you now enjoy. May I pray with you one more time as you begin to see things in a brand-new way?

> Father, like what happens when we open windows on a beautiful spring day, please let your light reflect upon the good things, small and big, in our lives. Thank you for the things we take for granted. Thank you for food and shelter and friends and family. Thank you for every breath, the ability to smell, the sights all of us walk right past every day. Today, help us choose to slow down and notice those good things. Please ignite a spark in our souls, and then set them on fire with gratitude and joy.

~

Again they cried openly. Orpah kissed her mother-in-law good-bye; but Ruth embraced her and held on.

—Ruth 1:14

I remember when Vicci and Suzie were little and an old girlfriend called me. She said my ex-husband and his new wife were at her house and wanted me to bring my children so his new wife could see them. Their biological father hadn't been involved in their life at all.

My husband said if he wanted to pay back child support and visit on a regular basis, then we would set up a visitation schedule.

I went to my girlfriend's house without the girls. My ex-husband was very cocky and said, "Where are my kids?" I told him he couldn't see the girls until he began to act like a father. He argued, but I told him no again because I didn't want him showing up every two or three years with no notice and arms full of gifts saying, "Here's your daddy."

So the girls grew up not knowing their biological father.

Chapter Seven

Setting Boundaries

"You have cancer."

When I had arrived at my yearly doctor's appointment, I had casually mentioned the lump. I'd found it while sleeping on a hard cot while being a counselor at a kids' camp. I wasn't concerned because I'd had two other small benign tumors removed in the past. I wasn't prepared for the quick trip to the radiologist for X-rays or the sober look on my doctor's face when he pronounced the early diagnosis.

I had just celebrated my thirty-second birthday. I was happily married. My three beautiful children were 8, 8, and 9 years old. I worked at a local engineering firm and took summers off with my children. I attended a night class once a week. I served as a youth sponsor and Sunday-school teacher. I was a sports mom. Between home, school, work, sporting events, volunteering, and church, my life was packed. I didn't know how cancer would fit in to my schedule.

From that time forward I became a "survivor" of a whole different kind. Friends and acquaintances came together to support us during that time. But an odd phenomenon occurred as well. Friends, family, and even strangers started telling me stories. They usually began something like this:

"Suzie, I heard the news and I just want to encourage you."

That was a great start, and I would listen with a grateful heart, until I realized many of the "encouraging" stories went something like this: "My Uncle Bob / Aunt Sarah / nephew Benjamin / neighbor Stu had cancer, and it was a glorious battle. He / she was courageous to the very end." These stories often included gruesome details about their uncle's /sister's / boyfriend's / cousin's struggle with the disease. Invariably the punch line involved pain medication, surgeries and more, and death— and fear would gravitate to the pit of my stomach. The person would walk away, but the story would linger long after their departure.

The statistics were challenging enough on their own. The odds we were given were, at best, a 40-percent chance of my surviving five years after undergoing aggressive chemotherapy, radiation, and surgery. At one time, we were given a 10-percent chance. Now, I had determined our fight against cancer would be launched with both faith and knowledge. I studied nutrition and various therapies. I prepared for surgery, chemo, and radiation by taking care of myself physically and spiritually. I spent time praying alone and found strength in God's presence.

But I didn't know how to handle the stories. One notable day I spent over an hour recovering and reflecting in a quiet place alone with God after a particularly vivid story. It was time to draw boundaries. The motivation behind people's "encouragement" was pure, but until I put out a signal, the stories weren't going to stop anytime soon.

What We Did

I enlisted my husband's help, and we discussed reasonable boundaries. If a conversation started the slip-and-slide descent toward discouragement or fear, he or I would subtly change the subject to something more hopeful. But that didn't always work. Though I understood the boundaries myself, I had not taken the time to share them with my friends and family. That was our next step.

It was uncomfortable the first time I stopped a friend at the beginning of a story. "I love it that you want to encourage me, but hearing about people who have died is really hard right now. I'm aware of the risks and possibilities, but I need you to help me in different ways."

"You've got it. What can I do?" she replied.

I shared with my friend specific things that really helped: prayer. Going to lunch. Telling me dumb jokes. Talking with me about all the things I loved before I heard the diagnosis of cancer.

My friend wrapped her arms around me and thanked me. "I honestly didn't realize the effect of what I was saying," she explained. "I just didn't know the right words to say."

It was a wonderful discussion. She understood that my life revolved around cancer at that time and that I was inundated with information about side effects and treatment options and survival stats almost daily. I realized my friend wanted to help, but had just entered new territory—having a friend diagnosed with a disease.

"If you have questions, ask me. If I really need a shoulder to lean on or even to cry on, I know you'll be there for me," I said. "And I'll ask you. I promise."

Once I shared the boundaries, 99 percent of my friends and family happily stopped the tales of "encouragement." Surprisingly, a small minority was offended.

"You've got to face the facts," one person said.

"You can't just pretend cancer doesn't exist," an acquaintance replied. When I explained I heard about cancer almost daily, this woman walked away miffed.

My old self—the one that depended upon others for my self-approval—would have cringed at her words. But setting boundaries was necessary. If I proposed them with tact and love and they weren't received, that was the other person's decision.

I was glad about the way most of my friends and family responded. One friend brought a hilarious poster and stuck it to the wall of my hospital room. Another friend picked up my children and took them to the movies or out to eat. One friend sat with me during chemotherapy sessions, and her company was not only comforting, but fun. We talked about our children and our husbands and our lives while the chemo pumped through my veins. One day she brought a silly hairpiece because our discussion the day before had revolved around wigs I might wear. While these kinds of gestures might have seemed inappropriate in light of the seriousness of my diagnosis—and may have been wrong for another person—they were just what the doctor ordered for me.

Setting boundaries wasn't easy, but it allowed me to let my loved ones know what I needed during that difficult time.

~

"Do you think I was wrong to keep your father out of your life?" the e-mail read.

My message jetted back to my mother. "No, I don't. I'm thankful that you and Dad set boundaries."

Those boundaries protected two little girls who didn't have the maturity to choose for themselves. My parents were willing to share the role of parenting with my biological father, but only after having agreed upon child support, regular visitation, and acknowledgment of important days like birthdays and holidays. By their setting limitations, the options became his. He was not shut out of a relationship with his children by anything other than his own choices.

We live within boundaries every single day. Personal boundaries keep me from eating four candy bars a day, because it's unhealthy in the long run. You may choose not to watch 20 hours of TV a week because there are more productive and life-enhancing activities to pursue. Lawbreakers receive consequences when they cross boundaries and hurt others for personal gain. Speed limits keep us from driving 60 miles per hour in a school zone. I push against the boundaries sometimes, but mostly I'm grateful for them.

One summer I traveled to a South American country with a group of young adults to restore a rescue house. Each day I braced for the commute, which resembled a giant game of chicken. It wasn't out of the ordinary to turn a corner only to see a mass of vehicles driving directly toward you. There were four distinct traffic lanes, two in each direction, but when motorists tired of waiting, they spilled over from their own two lanes into a third. The laws of the land were totally ignored. Every day we saw numerous wrecked vehicles at the side of the road, many with injured drivers and passengers. The day we arrived home, I wanted to kiss the ground because I had a newfound appreciation for traffic laws and for those who enforce them.

A Problem and a Solution

If I can't acknowledge my needs, why should others?

Anonymous

Drawing boundaries is necessary when a depressed, addicted, or mentally unstable parent or person continues to affect you and your family adversely. Many people are not conscious that they are being selfish, hurtful, or abusive. It's a pattern of behavior they've adopted, and it works for them as long as no one contests it. Boundaries are an invitation to change the current relational dynamics through...

1. acknowledging the problem
2. offering mutual guidelines that could result in reconciliation or resolve the issue
3. understanding that when behaviors are merely excused,

it encourages the person to continue in the same
pattern

Acknowledging the problem is often the most difficult step. One example is that of adults who grew up in an alcoholic household. They learned from an early age that talking about the problem results in relationship ramifications. Life goes on as "normal" while the disease rules the house. Children intercept phone calls, miss school events, and make excuses. They rarely address the effects of alcoholism because there is a price to pay if they do, such as emotional outbursts, accusations, or chaos.

As children they learn to remain silent—in a carefully orchestrated dance where addiction takes the child by the hand and waltzes into further dysfunction and despair. However, if you're an adult and your parent is still exhibiting destructive behavior, you are not required to continue the dance. Setting boundaries is an act of wholeness and can lead to winning for both parties. Creating mutual guidelines says that you will not allow your parents' choices to alter your life or the lives of your children any longer. You demonstrate to them through boundaries the healthy way to treat you and others.

Before you set boundaries, it's crucial you understand what they are not. Establishing boundaries is not being legalistic. The intent is not to fix, punish, or control another person. Boundaries are not intended to end relationships, but to conserve and deepen them.

People who have had a hard time setting boundaries often go from one extreme to the other. They leap from no boundaries to setting rigid limits. They move from silence to ultimatums. Boundaries go both ways, however. You have permission to request proper treatment for you and your family, but also to offer healing behavior in return. A few years ago I watched a late-night cultural debate. The talk show guests included a celebrity, a nationally known journalist, a well-known pastor, and a politician. Opinions flew around the room, and soon the discussion grew heated. The pastor offered his opinion. The celebrity stood to her feet and shouted, "Don't you dare talk to me like that! You better show respect!" She called him names, slurred his belief system, and interrupted him when he tried to clarify his stand gently. Communication broke down because the boundaries were one-sided.

Guidelines to Get You Started

As you develop boundaries, think of them as a two-way street. I suggest the following guidelines to reveal clear expectations for both parties. The first four are mutual guidelines.

1. We will treat each other with honor and respect.
2. The words of our mouths will not harm each other.
3. We will be honest in our relationship. We will not lie or deceive one another.
4. We will not take advantage of each other.

The last six boundaries are designed specifically for your relationship with a dysfunctional loved one.

5. I will always tell the truth—I won't pretend you aren't addicted, ill, or unstable.
6. I will support you with love and encouragement; however, I will not enable you.
7. I will allow you to take responsibility for your actions. I won't cover or fix your problems with money, in the court system, or with other people.
8. I am available to listen, but not when you are trying to shift blame for your actions on others. I will live out an example, and I won't shift blame upon you or others for my actions.

9. I will take threats of suicide or criminal acts seriously and will report them so you can receive help.

10. If your behavior or words endanger my children physically or emotionally, I will do what is reasonable to keep them and their environment safe.

So where do you begin? It's important that when you set boundaries you don't set them without warning, and that you provide an alternative. The other person has ingrained behavioral patterns. If a father is used to demanding his way and receiving instant compliance because he is verbally aggressive, boundaries will upset his expectations. He is used to shouting and having people move to comply. Your mutual guideline in that instance is "We will respect each other." A reasonable way of applying that guideline is to say "Please ask me instead of making an ultimatum," or "It's important to me that we talk as adults, rather than as parent and child." Progress may come slowly or not at all, but remember, whether mutual progress comes or not, setting boundaries is showing others your needs.

The Benefits of Follow-Up

If the other person doesn't comply, then you exercise reasonable consequences. If a father understands that when he shouts and is verbally abusive, his daughter and her family will quietly leave (showing tact and respect as they do so), his behavior is revealed with dignity. This action is not intended to punish him, but to facilitate a healthier way for him to communicate with his loved ones. When the situation doesn't escalate into verbal wars and the daughter holds fast to the guideline of mutual respect, the father is left to consider his actions and develop alternative ways to communicate at the next visit. If the consequences are consistent, soon he may realize that every time he berates a family member, he loses an opportunity to be with his family.

Sharing your needs allows you to be sensitive to the needs of others. A few years ago my younger sister stopped me after a visit. We had enjoyed a fun day together. "Sis, I need something from you," she said. "I need a hug when I leave. I don't get to see you very much, and it's important to me."

Mindy isn't an emotionally needy woman. She's bright, smart, and confident, and she was brave enough to let me know there was something I wasn't giving her. I didn't realize how important it was. Every time I see her now, I give her a warm hug. When she's leaving, I let her know I love her.

We've learned to communicate our needs in a positive way.

What happens when mutual guidelines are not honored? A loved one might get angry or refuse to respect boundaries. If they are addicted or unstable, they may be unreasonable. These are very real possibilities, and consistency on your part is key because you are the healthy one.

There will be times you will have to walk away rather than be drawn into futile arguing. When they test you to see if you mean what you say, you will have to follow through. You must be strong enough to step back so they can assume responsibility for their choices or behavior. If you don't, they may never clearly see their need for help or change. If you do, it just might be a catalyst to help your relationship be restored to health.

***

Setting boundaries does not mean that you develop a rigid set of rules to hand out to your family, friends, and co-workers. Setting boundaries is about having the courage to share what you need with a measure of grace. Let's take a few minutes and examine this topic of boundaries further.

1. Do you need to set boundaries with a still-dysfunctional loved one? Have you set them? Why or why not?

   _____

   _____

   _____

   _____

2. Do you feel guilty setting boundaries? List the reasons why.

   _____

   _____

   _____

   _____

3. Does that guilt enable destructive behavior on their part or keep the relationship unhealthy?

   _____

   _____

   _____

   _____

4. List two mutual guidelines for this relationship. They can be taken from the list, or you can create your own. (Keep in mind what boundaries are, and what they are not.)

   _____

   _____

_____

_____

5. Examine the six boundaries for still-dysfunctional relationships. Which apply to your situation?

_____

_____

_____

_____

6. Are you prepared for this other person to be angry with you if you set boundaries? Name one reason why you love them enough to let them be angry. What is your motive?

_____

_____

_____

_____

7. How will you respond if they are angry? Plan this in advance. Keep in mind the mutual guidelines.

_____

_____

_____

_____

8. List two alternatives for responding (for example, "Instead of calling me names, I need you to talk with me without labels."). When

would be a good opportunity to share these with your loved one who is involved in destructive behavior?

_____

_____

_____

_____

9. If your loved one chooses *not* to share the mutual guidelines, what is a reasonable response or consequence? (Remember, boundaries and consequences are not to fix, punish, or control, but to conserve and deepen relationships.)

_____

_____

_____

_____

10. Think of who can help you be consistent in applying reasonable boundaries—perhaps a friend or your spouse—and list their name(s). Plan a time to ask them to help you in your resolve.

_____

_____

_____

_____

After thinking through these questions, perhaps this is your prayer:

> Lord, thank you for the strength and wisdom to set boundaries. You love me enough to set guidelines for my life, such as integrity, joy, peace, self-control, goodness. Thank you that you guide me to live a life that is higher, and designed with purpose. Help me to know when to set boundaries. Help me to be real about my needs. Help me to see others' needs. I don't want to hide secrets or my feelings anymore. I know this won't be easy, but thank you for the strength of the Holy Spirit to do what is right for me, my family, and my relationships.

∿

Don't fret or worry. Instead of worrying, pray. Let petitions and praises shape your worries into prayers, letting God know your concerns. Before you know it, a sense of God's wholeness, everything coming together for good, will come and settle you down. It's wonderful what happens when Christ displaces worry at the center of your life.

—Philippians 4:6-7

Though I can't undo the things I did to my children, I decided a long time ago to become someone my children can love and respect. My children mean the world to me. They are my whole life. I thank God for them each day, but it took me quite a few years to learn that I was someone special in God's eyes.

Anytime we give love to others, whether they receive it or not, it rewards us with joy. My healing process began as I began to give that to myself.

Chapter Eight

Breaking Down Walls

"So, how are things going?" my friend asked.

"Richard hates shift work. He's really struggling with the changing hours."

My friend and I met three times a week to swim at the Y. We were on a pursuit to find the sleek bodies we knew existed under our post-baby selves. My friend's mother joined us that morning, and we swam laps up and down the length of the pool. We stopped to take a breather, though we were far short of our Olympian goal, and trod water as we talked. My friend and I were used to swimming deep not only in the pool—we also scuba dived into the daily details of our lives, not hesitating to talk about life in general.

My friend's mother joined us at the side of the pool. She was unusually quiet and seemed slightly uncomfortable. I attempted to draw her out. "What about you? How are things going with you?"

Water splashed me in the face as the older woman turned and swam away, her feet kicking furiously.

"Did I do something wrong?" I asked, confused.

My friend shrugged. "No, she just doesn't let people in, that's all."

Her mother swam toward the end of the pool and climbed out. As she sat on the edge of the pool and dangled her feet in the water, my friend and I silently began another lap.

My heart was heavy. What events had taken place in this woman's life to make her build such high, impenetrable walls? Then I remembered back to when I used to hide behind walls of my own.

∾

I was 15 years old. My friend asked me to come to church with her. I told her no, but she continued to ask. I finally went with her, hoping she might leave me alone after that. I sat in the small church and watched the people around me. In spite of myself, I was intrigued. The minister put away his guitar and opened his Bible. He shared a sermon. He said that God loved each one of us. I slipped out of my pew and started for the back of the church. I was prepared to walk home.

So, where was he, this God? Why wasn't he paying attention to what was going on in my home? Couldn't he see I was hurting? Had he noticed my little brothers hiding in the closet when life got scary? Did he watch my older sister leave home at 16, never to return? A tear slipped down my cheek, and I swiped it away. I was too tough to cry.

God, are you real? It was a question I had never asked, but somehow in that place and at that time, it made sense. I didn't ask out of reverence, but out of anger and hurt so raw that I challenged God. I ventured out of my self-constructed walls for just a moment to spar with the Maker of the universe.

It was a risky endeavor. It was much safer on the inside of my fortress. I had carefully constructed my walls: *Never let them see you cry. Pretend it doesn't hurt and crack jokes, and it will all go away. Hang on for three more years until you graduate, and then you'll be free to make your own decisions.*

The bricks layered higher and higher around my heart. There was room for only me inside that wall, but in my thinking God wasn't real, so it didn't matter if I opened up a little chink just to check.

I expected absolutely nothing. But God's gentle touch slipped past my awkward defenses and brushed my heart. I didn't see him. The heavens didn't open up. Nothing tangible occurred, but that day I received a great gift—I sensed God's presence for the first time. He was not only real, but somehow he knew and loved me. He drilled a hole in the wall around my heart. I reached out through that tiny opening as he brushed my fingertips, and I sensed freedom for the first time.

Though nothing appeared to have changed on the outside of my life, everything was different on the inside of me. It was the day my walls started tumbling down.

Possibilities for a Brand-New Day

General Secretary Gorbachev, if you seek peace,
if you seek prosperity for the Soviet Union and
Eastern Europe, if you seek liberalization:
Come here to this gate! Mr. Gorbachev, open this gate!
Mr. Gorbachev, tear down this wall!

PRESIDENT RONALD REAGAN, JUNE 12, 1987

Till August 11, 1961, half a million people crossed the border daily between East and West Berlin. Many from the East shopped and worked in the West, and vice versa. There were friends and families on both sides. On August 12, the East German army, police, and *Kampfgruppen* shut down the city and built a wall in the darkness of night. Loved ones and friends were separated. They lost not only physical contact with family and friends, but also their careers and the ability to visit their favorite shops, restaurants, and theaters. The concrete wall divided once-busy streets and railways. Stations were closed. Nothing was spared, not even cemeteries. It wasn't impossible to cross the wall, but it was danger-ous, difficult, and sometimes deadly. Armed guards protected the wall fiercely, and people stayed away.

Twenty-eight years later, in November 1989, a traffic jam formed on both sides of the wall as thousands drove from their homes to see if what they had heard was true. They opened their car windows despite the brilliantly cold night, and everyone talked to each other. People danced as musicians played their violins in the street. They climbed up in trees, on signs, and on buildings to wave and shout. TV cameras and reporters stood in the crowd and filmed everything.

The guard towers on both sides of the border were empty and the barbed wire was shoved aside. Giant drills punched holes in the wall. Every time a drill poked through the concrete, people cheered. Many grabbed hammers and chipped away with all their might. When a hole was created, hands thrust through and touched fingertips on the other side. Cranes lifted slabs of concrete, and hundreds of people jumped onto the wall. Many waved flags. People helped each other, lifting and pulling them up to climb to the other side. Joy erupted as men and women swarmed from one side to the other. This eventful night signaled the end of one era and the beginning of a brand-new day in history.

In *The Self-Confident Woman,* Janet Congo writes, "Each of us is an ever-growing, changing, and becoming individual."[15] To be such an individual in the fullest sense, we must deal with the walls in our lives. Emotional walls separate you from people, from your purpose, and from living fully. Years ago I should have carried a tool pocket on my belt because it was as if I needed a hammer around every corner. I continually encountered walls that needed to be smashed so I could become the person I wanted to be. Sometimes I chipped away at a wall, and other times I swung a sledgehammer to demolish the barriers between me and wholeness.

How Walls Look and What They Do

Emotional walls are of many kinds. A wall might be the controlling behavior or addiction that numbs you and keeps your feelings suppressed. A wall might be your workaholic hours or the pursuit of a career or success above any other element in your life. It could be avoidance of anything personal or intimate. Though walls appear in different forms, their purpose is always to keep people away.

The funny thing about walls is, they often look nice on the outside.

We dress them up, masking them with a smile, with politeness, or a polished exterior. We might even win awards for our walls, but underneath the facade, a cracked fortress resides around our heart and soul. As women, we are perhaps the finest craftsmen of walls. They serve as shelter; as long as we remain inside we avoid further hurt or exposure. They mask vulnerability. The armed guard at the wall is you because that is the only person you trust.

On rare occasions someone will get past, but it is difficult and even dangerous. They are tested at every juncture and, if they fail, the sentry removes them and locks the door. There are very few second chances.

You do realize you could open up to possibilities or new beginnings, but removing the walls also leaves you defenseless, and that is too great a price to pay. Perhaps your greatest fear might be exposed: *Will they see me for who I really am?*

Uncovering New Opportunities

Living without walls is not without risks, but residing in an emotionally closed off world has its own dreadful consequence: *It's lonely in there.* May I present three more truths at this point in your healing?

1. You might get hurt when you tear down the walls around your heart, but you also open the door to new possibilities.

2. Breaking down walls will allow you to give and receive love freely.

3. There are people from your past who are hiding behind their own walls and have become imprisoned.

In my office, there is a picture on my desk of my mom and me. We love flea markets! We were on a search that day for a vintage treasure. I especially love old costume jewelry—brooches, bracelets, and fun and funky pieces from great-grandma's time. As I study the photo, though, I see riches of a very different nature. My arm is around my mom's shoulder. We are smiling, and it is genuine. A passerby might think it is just an ordinary family photo, but I see two women who dared to let down their walls and venture over them to begin a stronger, healthier relationship. My mother allowed herself a new beginning. I discovered there was more to my mother and our relationship than my childhood.

As I tore down these and other walls, I discovered a maze of smaller barricades in the way. I had to knock down resentment, anger, bitterness, unforgiveness, and hurt. Sometimes I thought I had overcome an issue, only to find another barrier ready to spring up in my heart as I turned a corner. Another wall—but also another opportunity to deal with it and learn.

"We live, we make mistakes, we suffer, and we learn," says Janet Congo. "Out of that pain we claim Philippians 1:6; growth, strength, and direction results. The greatest tragedy comes when we don't learn."[16] Every time a brick fell down in my life, I felt like dancing because I had learned something new. My thought life was transformed. I started to believe things could be different. I learned that if I wasn't open to the possibilities outside the wall I missed much more than I gained. The first chip in the wall was when I allowed God to join me inside. He knew me. He wasn't afraid of the anger in my heart. He helped me to climb over to the other side to explore the possibilities.

He still is.

Perhaps that is your first step to tearing down the emotional walls—to invite him in. You are safe when you are vulnerable with your heavenly Father. He won't take advantage of your invitation. He's been waiting for you to ask him to join you. He will help you find your way out.

There were times when a piece would break off of my walls and I would feel naked. I felt people could see me—the real me, flawed and tenderhearted and messy. What would people do with what used to be hidden? It was a trust issue—but I can't control what others do, and I wanted to live life fully—so I stood naked.

I gave myself permission to love fully and to accept love from imperfect people. I don't ask for more than they can give and if they don't give what I need, I look to my Savior. He is my need-meeter.

Are you ready to chip away at a wall in your life?

1. Do you consider yourself to be an "ever-growing, changing, and becoming individual"? What does such a person look like?

_____

_____

_____

_____

2. Name the wall you have erected around your heart. Describe how it keeps others out.

_____

_____

_____

_____

3. What do you gain by living behind this wall? What have you lost?

_____

_____

_____

_____

4. Have you ever let anyone in, only to push them back out? Why?

    _____

    _____

    _____

    _____

5. Which tool that you've learned about (studying generational patterns, forgiving, boundaries, and so forth) seems most helpful for chipping away at that barrier?

    _____

    _____

    _____

    _____

6. Are you willing to risk vulnerability? What is your greatest fear about that? What do you hope might occur in your life?

    _____

    _____

    _____

    _____

7. There are numerous benefits to breaking down walls. Possible benefits include maturity, compassion, forgiveness, emotional freedom, and the ability to be genuine. Is it worth it to be naked or vulnerable to attain these? Share your thoughts about this.

    _____

_____

_____

_____

8. What's the difference between setting boundaries and tearing down walls? How do boundaries empower relationships, while walls divide?

_____

_____

_____

Father, I dance with my friend today as she picks up the hammer and chips away at the walls that have kept her from living fully. I'm glad she is not alone, not emotionally naked, because you clothe her with your purpose and with life that is full and wonderful. Thank you for new beginnings and new possibilities, and for a brand-new era in her life.

∾

There has never been the slightest doubt in my mind that the God who started this great work in you would keep at it and bring it to a flourishing finish on the very day Christ Jesus appears.

—Philippians 1:6

I still have a lot of fears because I don't know all the things people learn in school. But I read at least five books a week. I know many people don't have proper English or spelling skills, and they finished school. But I still struggle. I know these things are trivial, but I envy others who know how to write proper sentences.

Do I think I'm dumb? No. I've accomplished many things. My dad once told me that you're never too old to learn. I learn new things every day. I can sew, crochet, knit, and paint, and I'm always learning new things on the computer. But sometimes I'm ill at ease with people I don't know. That's my own hang-up. I think they might hear me speak poor English. I find myself holding back.

I think I could be like my girls, laughing so hard and having fun. I would like to be like that.

CHAPTER NINE

Becoming a Risk-Taker

"Whoosh, whoosh, whoosh."

"Good job! Now take a deep cleansing breath."

The room was packed with oversized bellies. Twenty-five pregnant women rested on mats while their significant others rubbed their backs. I practiced breathing while trying not to giggle at the ridiculous picture of myself panting and pushing in rhythm with the rest of the pregnant Lamaze choir.

A young blond woman looked my way and smiled. She was truly beautiful. The excitement of upcoming motherhood was evident on her face. I had met her at the first class briefly. I couldn't remember her name, but she was bubbly and outgoing and could out-talk anyone I had ever met. My husband leaned down and interrupted my thoughts. "What about getting together with that couple after class? They seem really nice."

"No." My answer was quick.

I sensed his disappointment, but I couldn't help it. Meeting people I didn't know was difficult for me.

Richard persevered. "Let's just go somewhere and get something to eat with them. You liked her. They might turn out to be great friends. Come on, Suz."

It was one of many such conversations we had in our first few years of marriage. It was a challenge being married to a person who'd never met a stranger, though Richard's outgoing personality is what had drawn me to him in the beginning. He saw me driving with a friend at college and followed us to a local fast-food restaurant. The next day he walked by me in the cafeteria and gently tweaked my cheek. That night he came by and threw rocks at my window to get my attention. He was persistent, and I fell in love with his bold but sweet overtures. He was Mr. Personality and wasn't afraid to show affection.

But after we married, Richard faced the challenge of being married to a woman who struggled with meeting new people. It wasn't shyness, because with friends and family I was open, but letting others into that circle of intimacy wasn't easy. It was one of my walls.

My worst fear was sitting in a room with a bunch of strangers and having nothing to say. I lacked confidence, and I recognized the problem, but I wasn't sure how to get past it. That night at the Lamaze class, Richard was true to his nature and persisted. I was thankful to leave the push-and-pant exercises behind, but I wasn't looking forward to climbing out of my comfort zone again. I hoped the couple would say no or they would have something more important to do. That hope was dashed when I heard the blond-haired girl respond just as quickly as I had.

"Sure!" she said. "I was hoping you would ask. We'd love to hang out."

We arrived at the restaurant and climbed into the booth, moving our large bellies with as much grace as possible into the small space. The pretty woman held out her hand.

"Hi! My name is Faith."

~

Faith was distraught. I assured her that Melissa had been so caught up in her wedding ceremony that she didn't know Faith and her family weren't in the church, but my best friend wouldn't be comforted. She loved Melissa as if she were her own daughter. She grieved that she had missed the big day due to an unexpected turn of events.

I decided to give my friend a surprise after-wedding party. I carried two pieces of wedding cake, mints and punch, rose petals, and a DVD of the wedding up the driveway to her home. Faith met me at the door, and when she saw what I had with me she flashed a huge smile and wrapped her arms around me.

"I love you!" she said.

We cut the cake and piled on the mints and nuts and poured our punch. Faith curled up in her brown leather chair and pressed a tissue to her eyes before the big show even began. The video started, and at the image of my daughter walking down the aisle on her father's arm, tears slid down Faith's cheeks.

"Oh my goodness, Suzie. She's so beautiful!"

Typical Faith. It's one thing I love about her. Her honesty and enthusiasm have been a part of my life for more than two decades now. The babies we carried when we first met are all grown up. Most of the six children (three for her, three for me) are out of the nest, but our friendship is ongoing. Our families have traveled together, played together, and worked side by side through good and bad times. We've supported each other through crises and major family events for the last quarter of a century.

It was Faith who was first on the scene when I discovered I had cancer. As I emerged from the haze of anesthesia after a segmented mastectomy, I heard someone talking nonstop. Faith was holding my hand. Her bright cheerful voice was just as powerful as the drugs in my system. She was also the person who hit the drug-dispensing button too many times (because I was moaning in my sleep) and helped me discover I was allergic to morphine. I woke up swollen like a sausage. It was just one more memory to add to the collection.

If I hadn't taken the risk 24 years ago (though admittedly with gentle but persistent persuasion), I would have missed out on a beautiful friendship.

My relationship with Faith was only the beginning of my adventures. No one has to nudge me anymore, because I've discovered the possibilities that come from taking personal risks far outweigh my fears.

I am officially a risk-taker.

"Do It Afraid"

> *Life isn't about weathering the storms.*
> *It's about learning how to dance in the rain.*
>
> ANONYMOUS

"Do it afraid."

I live by these words. They are ingrained in my heart and spirit. I follow their advice often. When I think about the 22-year-old young woman who preferred to stay in her safety zone, I don't recognize her anymore. I still struggle at times, but only because I'm taking bigger steps, larger calculated risks. I've learned the truth of what Erwin McManus says:

> We are seldom afraid when our opposition is smaller than us. When we keep our challenges manageable, we not only manage our fear, but squelch our faith. One way to deal with our fears is to surround ourselves with security and predictability. We may look courageous when in fact all we've done is minimize our risk.[17]

The first time I spoke to a women's group, it was frightening—but I was no longer content to remain in a safety zone. Doors started to open, and I vowed to step through each one, no matter how uncertain I might be. Today when I stand in front of crowds at national conferences, "Do it afraid" is still uppermost in my mind. I may not score 100 percent in my abilities, talents, and personality—or with other people—but the good news is that I'm not striving for perfection or even acceptance. I just want to move forward as a woman and discover who I can be.

Speaking was only one risk. Taking off the mask to be myself with other women was another. I once struggled with the fact that I don't like what most women love. I don't own a glue gun because I burn myself every time! I don't like to shop even when I can afford to, though I love fun clothes and jewelry and especially shoes. I don't collect things because that means I have to dust them. I love go-carts and hiking and riding horses. I love the water, and I love skiing and tubing on it and riding in a boat with water splashing my face. (I will never understand why some women go to a swimming pool and don't get their hair wet.)

Calculated Risks

In light of what I've said, may I present three more principles to consider:

1. You don't have to try to be anyone but yourself.
2. When you accept who you are, you are more accepting of others.
3. When you take calculated risks, you discover talents and facets of your personality waiting to be developed.

The benefit of taking off the mask is that you discover there are lots of women just like you. Many women have cornered me after a conference and hugged me, saying, "I'm so thankful you shared that." You see, they too were thinking there was one mold that we all fit in, and if they were outside that cookie-cutter mold, something was wrong with them. Accepting who I am allows me to fully accept my girlfriends who love to drink tea, who buy swimsuits that will never get wet, and who ooh and aah over their collection of Precious Moments figurines.

We can all just be ourselves.

To others, the payoff when you take calculated risks might not look like success, but every risk ignites courage. If you decide never to venture out of your comfort zone, you are fully safe—but also stuck. Planning and implementing calculated risks helps you discover the woman you are becoming. Every time you venture outside your comfort zone you discover something new about yourself. In the past 20 years, as I have peeled away layers, I've found out I can be comfortable in a circle of three or in front of a crowd of 5000. I've discovered that, though I'm quiet by nature, I can initiate and enjoy conversations with people I don't know. I've discovered that most women are looking for their next great friendship. I've pushed the edges of my safe world outward to learn, absorb, and attempt new things and to meet new people. Even if I fail, my confidence pool is filled to the brim because I continue to learn more about others and myself.

Where Do You Begin?

How do you begin taking calculated risks? The first step is to differentiate between a calculated risk and risky behavior. Risky behavior is hasty. It thrives on impulsive actions and is fed by feelings. It ignores long-term consequences and is performed without thought of the impact on yourself or others. For example, a woman who opens her heart to a man whose lifestyle will not nurture a relationship or honor her is exhibiting risky behavior. She chooses a temporary need for relationship over her long-term needs for stability, commitment, and respect. That's risky behavior.

A calculated risk is planned and has a specific goal. Calculated risks cost you something (thus the word "risk"), but you've weighed the cost versus the benefits and decided the possible advantages are worth it. Calculated risks are…

- running after your dreams and trying new things
- exploring talents that lie dormant

- reaching out to new friends and believing you can be accepted and valued for who you are

And especially a calculated risk is saying that, in spite of your past,

- you can be the mom your children need you to be—the mom you know is inside of you

This mom may not look or sound exactly like the woman next door. Your strength might not be baking cookies for the PTA—it might instead be playing on a summer day with your children and not caring how your hair looks. (But that doesn't stop you from tapping into the friendship of a neighbor as you make peanut-butter brownies together.) Or, you may be the best cook in town and have the talent to throw together the theme party of the century, but you aren't afraid to allow people to see you or your home when things aren't perfect.

Your calculated risk is believing you have something of value to offer the little (or big) ones living in your house. It's believing you have what it takes to nurture and shape your child. It's forgiving yourself when you err, because you are no longer striving to be the perfect mom—just a real woman loving her kids and growing every day as a mom and as a person.

But What If...

What stops a person from taking calculated risks? One word: *fear.* I found a definition of fear that made perfect sense:

False

Evidence

Appearing

Real

F.E.A.R. is the "what ifs." What if you unmask your emotions and can't control them? What if you tell your secrets and are rejected? What if someone glimpses the real you under the mask of perfection and finds a flawed human being?

But there are other "what ifs" to consider. What if you unmask your emotions and actually deal with them? What if you tell your secrets and they no longer suffocate you in the hidden places of your heart? What if you live in authenticity and discover new and lasting relationships (even with those in your own home)? What if you face your fears and overcome them? What if along the way you discover who you are and what you can do? These "what ifs" will allow you to rejoice in the new horizons as the boundaries are expanded.

There was a man in the Bible named Peter, who pushed the margins of his life. One stormy day he and friends were in a boat and Peter saw Jesus walking toward him on the water. He leaped out of the safety of the boat and started walking toward his friend. Though the waves whipped around him, he took several confident steps until F.E.A.R. overtook him.

What if he sank? What if the guys in the boat didn't jump in to save him? Why hadn't he grabbed a life jacket on the way out? He had a full-blown panic attack and cried out to Christ. Jesus took Peter by the hand and showed him that they could walk together through the turbulent waves.[18]

When some read this story, they call Peter's venture out of the boat a failure. After all, they point out, Peter sank.

But he also walked on water!

As you bravely knock down walls, the next step is to consider taking calculated risks. Remember when you were a child and your best friend dared you to climb the monkey bars? I dare you today to love imperfect people and to be real. I dare you to believe you are a woman who is gifted and beautiful and worthy. I dare you to forgive yourself when you fall short of that goal.

I dare you to believe that the way you grew up doesn't define who you are, and that you can give your children a different legacy. I dare you to take a risk and, even if it isn't 100-percent successful in the eyes of the world, to consider it an accomplishment.

You don't know what treasure you might find as you take calculated risks. It might be that a broken young woman who once saw herself in a distorted looking-glass self will discover exactly who she is—and like what she sees.

Each of these questions will help you figure out the difference between calculated risks and risky behavior. Weigh the costs versus the benefits and the motivation behind the risks. Don't let the risks you cannot take at this time eliminate the possibilities of those that you can.

Are you ready? Put on your parachute! You're about to take the first step—and fly as a risk-taker.

1. Using the example of the woman looking for love, define the difference between risky behavior and calculated risks.

    _____

    _____

    _____

    _____

2. Describe a time you engaged in risky behavior and the costs associated with it.

    _____

    _____

    _____

    _____

3. Would you consider taking a *calculated* risk even if the outcome might not be 100-percent successful? Name one calculated risk you are willing to take.

_____

_____

_____

_____

4. Name one benefit you would hope to gain as a result, both for you and your family.

_____

_____

_____

_____

5. What is your reaction to the idea of F.E.A.R. (false evidence appearing real)? Define the greatest case of F.E.A.R. in your life.

_____

_____

_____

_____

6. What is the worst thing that could happen if your F.E.A.R. came true? What is the best thing that could happen for you personally if you took the chance anyway? Which is greater?

_____

_____

_____

_____

7. What are the "what ifs" that keep you from taking risks in relationships?

_____

_____

_____

_____

8. What are the "what ifs" that keep you from taking risks in your
   personal life (risks such as discovering who you are and what you
   are capable of)?

_____

_____

_____

_____

9. Make a plan and include a timeline ("I will take step one by this
   date": _____). Journal your thoughts about the process. Are you
   afraid? Hopeful?

_____

_____

_____

_____

10. What is one calculated risk you can take as a mother? As a wife?

_____

_____

_____

_____

11. A friend of mine planned 50 new things to try before she turned 50 (she is in her 30s). Some of them are small, like eating a new type of food. Others are scary, like bungee-jumping. Some of them are educational, like reading a new book once a month. Others have to do with personal growth and trying new things to discover her passions (for example, sewing, speaking, journaling, scrapbooking, riding a horse). If you were to name five new things you want to try before your next birthday, what would they be?

_____

_____

_____

_____

It is time to "Do it afraid." As you take calculated risks to forgive, establish new patterns with your children and spouse (or ex-spouse), be vulnerable, and open your heart to new friendships and relationships, remember this: Every courageous man and woman in the Bible faced fear when called to greater things. They often looked at themselves and wondered what God was thinking. These were ordinary people with challenges. Moses stuttered. David was the sibling no one noticed. Caleb was afraid to take the next step. Mary was young and inexperienced.

But God wasn't looking for superheroes. He was looking for those who weren't afraid to trust in something greater than themselves. Don't be afraid to reach out to him and ask him to help you.

Will you consider making this your prayer today?

> Dear God, I am willing to climb out of this safe box I've fashioned for myself. I trust you. You have a plan for my life, don't you? I see you're taking me deeper in my friendship with you and leading me to a place of healing. Help me understand that courage is not expecting perfect results. Please take that pressure from me. In fact, Lord, I'm handing that pressure to you today, willingly, because it's not about what I will receive, but who I will become. Courage is not one single action but something we live day by day, isn't it? I'm delighted over who I am becoming as I take calculated risks. Thank you for taking me by the hand as I become a risk-taker.

∽

Peter, suddenly bold, said, "Master, if it's really you, call me to come to you on the water." He said, "Come ahead." Jumping out of the boat, Peter walked on the water to Jesus. But when he looked down at the waves churning beneath his feet, he lost his nerve and started to sink. He cried, "Master, save me!" Jesus didn't hesitate. He reached down and grabbed his hand.

—Matthew 14:28-31

Part Three:

Giving Your Kids the Gift of the Future

I learned that we can become the person God created—loving, joyful, happy, confident. We can reach out to others and love them, all the while feeling good about who we are. If I could talk with someone whose life is like mine once was, I would say that God is the great Healer. He can make you whole again, no matter how broken you once were. He can give you a new spirit on the inside of you. He can give you what you need to forgive the wrongs done to you, and he can give you what you need to forgive yourself for what you have done to others.

Don't waste one more day living in the past. Don't feed your bitterness. It only hurts you and your loved ones. Life is short. Start today by choosing happiness. God can do that for you.

When we're stuck in the past, feelings control our actions, thoughts, and words. It is all we have to nourish ourselves with because our souls are empty. We believe the negative thoughts. We don't know how to love ourselves, so we struggle with loving others. With those images in mind, we remain stagnated. We can't move forward until we let go of that hurt and those thoughts.

How do I know this? I am one of those people whose past is something I went through to get to where I am today.

CHAPTER TEN

Letting Go

"Let me get a good look at that rock!"

Melissa held out her hand to show off her brand-new engagement ring to my sister Mindy. My nieces, Meagan, Paige, and Kimberly, leaned in to get the scoop and to hear the details of the proposal. They snuggled on the couch, laughing and talking as their cousin shared the exciting news.

In the kitchen, my mom hummed an off-key version of a Christmas tune while she bustled about, cleaning up after our Thanksgiving feast. I smiled as I watched her load the plates she had just thoroughly washed into the dishwasher to "sanitize" them.

My dad lounged in his faded blue recliner and watched the football game with my husband and brothers. My younger nephews, Avery and Jason, played a game of cards at their feet. It was a typical family holiday scene.

As I watched the Norman Rockwell picture, I had to ask myself one question: *When did we become a typical family?*

~

It's funny how we trap people in time warps. It's just human nature. At a high-school reunion, I was eager to see old friends. As I walked up the sidewalk to Will Rogers High, I passed familiar strangers. Some of the men had thinning hair. Others carried some extra weight around their middle. Some of the women were pregnant, and little children surrounded many. As I walked through the metal doors, I felt as if I'd stepped back in time. I could almost smell the cafeteria food. I could hear the bell ringing and lockers clanging as kids ran to class.

I vividly remember the roles we played in our teen years and the labels we wore—all of which seem so out of place now. In the throes of adolescence, though, those labels held great significance for us. There were the jocks, the popular girls and guys, the cheerleaders, the nerds. I remember the girls and guys who always dressed in the latest trends and somehow missed the gawky, awkward stages that others battled. I recall the smart students who excelled in chemistry and trigonome-try. As I glanced at the people around me, the labels no longer fit in the adult world.

I loved high school. It was a fun—and sometimes painful—period of my life. I had a serious boyfriend for two years. He was cute, and we wrote long, promise-filled notes to each other in our yearbooks.

In high school I grew in my faith. I attended a small church and was active in the youth group. I zipped from home to home on Friday nights and looked forward to Sunday-night youth services and outreach ministry on Sunday afternoons. I have fond memories of piling into the bus and traveling to eat nachos and chocolate milkshakes. It was a Sunday tradition. When I wasn't busy with church things, I filled my Mustang with friends and we toilet-papered each other's homes.

I wasn't sure how many people from my old high school would even remember me. If they did recall Suzie Morrison, it might be a faint memory of a skinny girl who smiled big and said little. But the woman walking through the doors of Will Rogers High several years later was very different. I was excited to see people, to reconnect, and to make new friends.

Trapped in the Past

As the evening was winding down, a guy came up and introduced himself.

"Do you remember me?" he asked.

My first kiss.

The memories flooded in. It was eighth grade. During a football game, the lights suddenly flashed off, then on, then went out. I was sitting next to him. He was tall and thin, and I liked him as a friend—and maybe, possibly, more. When darkness enveloped the stadium, I felt cold lips hit mine. The encounter was unexpected. Kissing wasn't on my resume yet, and I didn't know what to do! Should I kiss back? Shriek? Grab him around the neck and see how long I could pucker?

But fear kicked in. I didn't move. My lips just sat there. After a few agonizing seconds, I pulled back. His lips hit my chin and slid off.

"You kiss like a fish," he said.

It was a sad ending to what could have been an almost romantic eighth-grade moment.

As he stood beside me, I smiled at that memory. I had almost forgotten it. For the next several minutes we stood there, and he shared humorous stories about the skinny girl he'd once known. After the fifth or sixth story, I tried to steer the conversation to family and friends. I hoped to talk about our adult lives, but he always directed the conversation back to the same track.

"So, where are you now?" I tried again. "What are you doing?"

"Do you remember..." he started, going right back to one more skinny joke, one more fish-lips moment.

It's not that I minded the stories. They *were* funny. Skinny jokes have definitely become a compliment, now that I've given birth to three children. But it felt odd to be stuck in a time warp. We remained two young thin adolescents on an aluminum bench trying our first kiss in the darkness.

After a while I slipped back to the table I'd been at earlier. I wasn't the shy, skinny Suzie he'd once called his friend, but all that he could see was the person I once was.

No one in that room that night was the same, though. Several of the "nerds" were handsome, successful businessmen and business-women. Some of the "jocks" were coaches, and others were men with bellies whose football glory days were a sweet memory. The homecoming queen was nine months pregnant with her second child. The cheer-leader was a working mom with two toddlers. We had all changed. I met new friends that night. Labels no longer mattered—and that's the beauty of adulthood. The shy, thin high-school girl was a part of me, but the woman who had fallen in love, given birth twice, gained weight, matured emotionally and spiritually—and who had discovered the joy of a really great kiss—was me as well.

Seeing in the Present Tense

I love you not only for what you are, but for what I am
when I am with you. I love you not only for what you have
made of yourself, but for what you are making of me.
I love you for the part of me that you bring out.

ELIZABETH BARRETT BROWNING

Just as I didn't wish to be remembered as nothing more than what I was as an eighth-grade girl, there are people all around us who don't want to be trapped in the roles they once played. Going back to the "Norman Rockwell" scene I described earlier, that was my challenge. As I traveled home that night from Thanksgiving dinner with my family, in my heart I fully grasped the miracles that God had performed, but I had to admit I had placed my family in a time warp.

I viewed them through the jagged pieces of my childhood, as if I were part woman, part child. At one point in the drive home, my daughter's fiancé leaned over the backseat.

"Your family is really great," he said.

Yes, they are, I thought.

I had one remaining step to take in my personal healing. It was time to completely move out of the past and let go of my bad memories so I could see my family in the present tense. Jennifer Kennedy Dean writes,

> As you learn to live in wholeness, you'll become more and more familiar with the reality of having to let go. Another word for that is relinquishment. It means, "leave behind; give up; release; to give over possession or control of." When you find the secret of relinquishment, you have come upon one of the most powerful weapons in the healing arsenal. I call this a weapon because many people mistakenly think of it as a weak or passive word. In its spiritual context, it is an aggressive and strong word.[19]

Letting go is sweeping the last remnants of regret, bitterness, remorse, and revenge out of your life. As I took this last step, a metamorphosis began in my heart. I no longer saw my family through the needs of the child I once was. I began to see *their* needs and hopes and dreams in addition to my own.

What were my mother's needs? One of them was to be accepted.

One night we waited together in an airport lobby. Mom clutched a teddy bear and a balloon. The person who was to arrive had heard the stories of the past. I could see hope—and concern—in my mother's face. Would she be accepted for who she was, or relegated to a role she had abandoned long ago? That visit was a success. That individual had the opportunity to see for herself who my mother had become and form a relationship based on what was now true in the present. And this relationship continues to grow.

Have you taken that last personal step? Before we begin to focus on our role in our children's lives, it is vital that you look at your extended family without interposing the filter of your childhood. What do you see?

Reconstructing Your Mental Pictures

I can't change how others view my mother, but I have reconstructed my mental picture of her to include the years that have passed. I have added subtle textures, such as her laugh. It was a sound we didn't hear much when we were children, but it's one I treasure now. I watch the woman who has become an artist. She paints fences and rocks and canvas. She splashes color wherever she is. I treasure the beautiful photographs she captures of sunsets in Canada.

I visited my mother and father one summer. I'm not an early riser, as I've already shared. I know that 5 AM exists, but I am almost never there to greet it. However, one certain morning was different. I woke up in the small back bedroom as Mom rustled around in the living room. I heard the sliding doors open and close. I sat up on the bed and watched her out the window. She quietly strolled to the edge of the lake and walked to a nearby craggy rock. She climbed up on it, rested on her back, and pointed her camera at the sky. As the sun crept along the horizon, she waited for the perfect moment and then snapped the picture. She remained there a few minutes longer as she snapped more photos. A tear ran down my face as I watched her. Deep inside of my mother is an eye for beauty. It has always been there, but I can see it clearly now.

Sometimes my mom still struggles. Throughout the writing of this book we had long conversations as she wrestled with the memories. I can only imagine how difficult it would be for me if the mistakes of my past were shared for the world to view. In one conversation, I told her I would stop the project rather than hurt her. After a few days she sent me a beautiful e-mail. She admitted that the week had proved difficult. She had questioned everything—herself, our relationship, how people would respond to this story. My offer to halt the project came because, if my story touched a hundred thousand women but brought pain to my mother, I didn't want to proceed.

At that point, it was time for her last step as well. It was time for her to let go of excuses, of guilt, of defense mechanisms. She faced the past squarely and acknowledged it for what it was—and then let it slip away as she grabbed tight to the truth. I loved her for that. I love who she has become.

She stepped into the present. She trusted who she had become. She felt acceptance, both from her daughter and from herself, and embraced it as her own.

As my mother has grown, a second need has developed in her. It is to be able to offer love to my brothers and sisters and me. It's the same desire I have for my own children. It's a universal desire.

Every time I return from my parents' home, I bring a bag with me from my mom. My children love to see what she's sent home. It might be magazines or a vintage coat from a thrift shop. It may be silverware or even a new broom. My mother loves matched sets and an organized household. I don't notice if the silverware matches—and if it's clean underneath, I'm happy. When she visits, she notes what I should have (matching silverware, washcloths that aren't five years old), and that might be my next gift.

One day I stopped her as she held out a bag of books.

"I don't need stuff, Mom. You are all I need."

"I just give it to you because I want to," she said.

I received another bag the next time I came. The gifts have little to do with silverware or magazines. Every time my mother puts something good into my hands, she is telling me she loves me. It's unspoken. The gifts aren't necessary, because all I truly want is my mother, but it is her way.

I in turn have learned to give her love in a way that makes sense to her. My mom's "love language" is time. When I help her learn a computer program or take her to dinner, she hears clearly "I love you." It would be easier to give her phone calls or send her gifts because time is something that seems to be always short. Yet time is honor. Even as I write this, I know I can offer her more time. Just small amounts make her happy. It's a gift to me as well.

Not Perfection, But a Process

Perhaps your parent has not made the healing progress that my mother has, and you struggle with letting go. Perhaps your parent is no longer alive, and you wonder how letting go of the bad family stories can help you in your healing journey. Letting go breaks the last thread holding you to the past. It doesn't change what happened. It doesn't necessarily change those who hurt you (though it can have a powerful effect on the relationship), but it does transform you. It shatters excuses, because you no longer see yourself as a victim. It gives you empathy, because you stand on the other side of healing. It allows you to respond with love and wisdom to those who are still healing or still broken.

Letting go has nothing to do with whether I have a picture-perfect family or not. I don't. One family member stays away, and our efforts to draw this loved one back have not been successful—yet. Each of us has made mistakes in our attempts to reconcile. These problems grieve not only me but every person involved because we all love each other in spite of fragmented relationships.

There are still disagreements from time to time in our extended family. There are moments when I see more than a hint of the emotional fragility we once feared in my mom. There are times I'm too straightforward—times I should keep my opinion to myself. But I urge you to consider these truths I've discovered as you let go of your bad family stories:

1. Every family experiences obstacles and bumps in the road, even *normal* families.

2. Healing is a lifelong process.

3. Your healing will impact others.

You'll never attain perfection. But that's exactly where you need to be—because when someone proclaims perfection, they stop the process. They've arrived—so they think—and there is nowhere greater to go.

I am hoping and believing for even greater things. When I look at my extended family, I don't see just "normal." I see a portrait of God's grace. We are still growing, still learning—and there are additional victories and challenges ahead. The paint on this portrait is still wet, and the brush is firmly in the master's hand.

As you read the following questions, answer them from the perspective of the confident adult woman you have become (or are becoming). Discard the filter of your childhood. Perhaps your loved ones have not grown or changed. If so, this chapter is still for you. The miracle is inside of you, and there is additional healing ahead as you take this step.

1. Describe a transformation that has taken place in a member of your extended family. Look for even the smallest of steps.

_____

_____

_____

_____

2. What is the greatest need in your family? What is God asking of you in that process?

_____

_____

_____

_____

3. If your family is still stuck in the same old harmful patterns, how do you wish to pray for them?

_____

_____

_____

_____

4. Do you feel that others trap you in past roles? Clearly define not only who you are now, but also how you wish to be viewed by those from your past. What part do you play in that?

_____

_____

_____

_____

5. Are you ready to let go of your bad family memories? What will you gain by focusing on the present rather than the past?

_____

_____

~

Tonight when the sky is clear and the stars are out, find a quiet place outside with God. As you view how large the universe is, I hope you will grasp that the hands that painted the sky are the hands of the One who will help you. He's right there with you. He's not small, and he's ready to help you so your healing can become a legacy to your children.

Heavenly Father, I'm ready now—ready to let go of the past. I don't want to filter the family stories through pain anymore. I will be truthful, but I won't put limits on what you can do for my family and for me. You were able to take my past and, through your grace, separate my wrong-doing from me as far as the east is from the west. Now, I want to give you my childhood and my family so you can sort out the bad from the good. I'm here before you as a woman on a journey to wholeness, and I'm taking you by the hand so you can help me find my way to that place. I release my future and let it fly as high as the stars and into your hands.

~

Forget about what's happened; don't keep going over old history. Be alert, be present. I'm about to do something brand-new. It's bursting out! Don't you see it? There it is! I'm making a road through the desert, rivers in the badlands.

—Isaiah 43:18-19

I feel like a mother my children can be proud of now. Sometimes I'm still a little bit afraid to let my guard down, but I'd like to think that there are new memories for all of us.

I would like to believe that my children will never take abuse from anyone. I pray they understand that my home is always their home and that if they ever need me, I'm there for them.

I don't know if I would be here today if I hadn't opened my life to God. He has shown me how to forgive others and forgive myself. He has taught me how to live with joy. He makes us whole again when we are broken. Because of his gift we can start over and find a renewed spirit and a new mind.

To know there is a way out of the past and into a bright, joy-filled, new future—that is joy unspeakable. To know I am still shaping my children's memories, but in a different way—that is a gift.

CHAPTER ELEVEN

Your Children's Memories

"If you could have lunch with three people from any time in history, who would it be?" asked Ryan.

"The president. Barbara Bush, because she has been both the wife and mother of a president. And Mother Teresa," I replied.

We play our own version of 20 Questions when we travel. My son, Ryan, is especially astute at asking questions that make you squirm, or at least make you think.

I asked my own question. "What is one thing you'll remember about me when I'm gone?"

"Your laugh."

"Definitely the laugh," Leslie said.

Melissa concurred.

My laugh? What about my killer chicken enchiladas or my sense of adventure? What about fun birthdays with homemade cake and a decorated birthday door? Wouldn't that be a great way to remember me? If I could pick one quality I *don't* want to be remembered for, it is my laugh. It's no ordinary chuckle. I get tickled easily at things that no one else finds funny. When I laugh, I often lose it. I've been known to laugh and cry for minutes while everybody else in the room giggles at *me*.

My younger sister is exactly the same way. Luckily for her, she passed it on to her daughter, and when all three of us are together, it's a riot. But my children seem to have a more sophisticated sense of humor.

When Melissa saw the surprised expression on my face, she said, "You know I love your laugh, Mom. It's one of the best things about you."

When Melissa was a little girl, each afternoon she flew off the school bus to talk about all the details of her day. This continued even after she left for college. Almost every day she called to tell us what was going on in her life. One day I realized our conversations weren't always private. She told a story about something that happened to a friend, and I erupted in laughter. She held up the phone and let her friends in the room listen. "See, I told you. There she goes," she said. I could hear the giggles of her college friends as they listened to Melissa's crazy mom.

When I think about the choices of memories that my children will one day sift through, perhaps laughter is not such a bad way to be remembered.

∼

The immensely famous song "Memories" from the movie *The Way We Were* reminds us that inside of each of us lie recollections from times gone by, a tapestry of fragrances and experiences and meaning-ful moments. What reminisces will come to mind for my children one day?

When my twins were still in diapers, two other women dropped by to visit. I was outside in the backyard of our small farmhouse. We'd made a huge batch of bubbles and splashed them on a long yellow Slip 'n' Slide. Summer was winding down, and the trees draped over our little oasis. I was in a swimsuit, sitting to catch the kids as they slid the length of the yellow strip and flew into my arms. The laughter was loud and contagious.

Nearby we had created a schoolhouse. Inside were crayons and paper and books, as well as snacks of juice and graham crackers. We had played in the schoolhouse for most of the morning and then cooled off in the water. It was a delightful day.

I stood up as the two visitors approached. One was a friend from church, and the other, a woman I had only recently met.

I had bubbles in my wet hair, and my makeup was washed away. Melissa had discarded her swimsuit and was wearing only a diaper. There were buckets of soapy water splashed everywhere. One woman walked carefully on the squishy grass.

"Can we come in?" one of them asked.

I thought about the mess in the house. There was a load of clean laundry on the rocker and another chair. Toys were scattered here and there. The breakfast dishes were rinsed but not washed. I had decided to play first, then to clean up while the little ones took their nap. I opened the door and let the guests in. One reached for Ryan, who was still wet, and carried him in. Leslie slipped and slid across the floor until she hit carpet. Melissa was sitting snugly on my hip, the place she seemed to love the best.

I offered my guests a choice of juice or milk, the only beverages we had. As I pulled out a towel and wrapped it around me to sit on the couch, one of the women looked around for a place. I set Melissa down and jumped up to move the clothes from the rocker to the chair.

"Sorry about the mess," I offered.

The first woman smiled, but the other said, "Well, if you can live with it, I can too."

I know she didn't mean harm, but suddenly I saw my inadequacies all around me. Somewhere in the world, maybe even in my own neighborhood, there was a woman who could raise three toddlers and change diapers and cook and keep an immaculate home. But it wasn't me.

The ladies stayed only a few moments and then left.

Spending Time, Not Wasting It

When I look back at that memory, I see it in a much different light than I did then. I recognize the overwhelming workload of a mother in her early 20s with three babies. I know she was sleep deprived and sometimes felt like a milk machine when her little ones were infants. I see her picking up toys and making meals and changing diapers. I see the mountain of laundry that eased only when the children left for college.

But I also see a woman who had fun with her children. Every day we woke up and schemed about the adventure we would have that day. It might be an hour at the local pool or a trip to the library or making cookies. It might be spraying shaving cream on the dining-room table and making pictures in the foam.

The truth is, we lived in a small home that wasn't equipped for a family of five, especially when three arrived in the space of 19 months. Keeping it clean was hard work —like mowing the grass and then going out five minutes later to see it regrown and needing to be mowed all over again. I tried very hard.

In hindsight I see that the times I delayed my housework for a couple of hours to hear my children's laughter weren't wasted moments. They are precious memories. The dishes and clothes that needed to be folded were there when we were through. We made picking up toys fun, racing against each other to see who could pick up the toys the fastest. My kids helped me make cookies and helped rinse dishes, standing beside me on chairs next to the sink.

When I was a young mother, older women sagely told me time would fly. At that time, knee-deep in diapers and nursing as I was, time seemed to crawl. It was measured in first steps and baby teeth and how many hours each child slept through the night. My memories of that time are wrapped around the smell of a baby's skin just after a bath; Ryan's deep baby laugh; my children playing on the floor with their daddy.

When they were a little older, I watched them play soccer and basketball and brought snacks to games. For several years, I would drive them to school and to practice and to church. My memories are of the smell of popcorn, of feeling as if I lived in a car, of watching Melissa jump around the house like a cricket when she was in gymnastics.

Then they were teenagers and learning how to drive and going on their first dates. My memories revolve around Leslie's harrowing driving lessons; the smell of Ryan's cologne; Melissa wearing a flowing white dress and homecoming crown; a house full of teenagers; and the smell of brownies baking.

Even then it seemed as if I had all the time in the world.

But I finally understand what these women were saying. They knew something I did not: We have a very limited time to shape our children's memories. One day my children will look back and recall the moments of their childhood.

I'm grateful that flying down a bubbly Slip 'n' Slide will be among those memories.

Your Influence

> *Kids have little computer bodies with disks that store information. They remember who had to do the dishes the last time you had spaghetti, who lost the knob off the TV set six years ago, who got punished for teasing the dog when he wasn't teasing the dog and who had to wear girls' boots the last time it snowed.*
>
> ERMA BOMBECK

Perhaps the ability to shape the memories of a child is the most powerful gift of parenthood and the one for which we should take the greatest responsibility. I have a box of snapshots I plan one day to organize, but it is the memories embedded in the minds of my children that will be handed from generation to generation.

In *High-Wire Mom,* Kendra Smiley describes her life as a watercolor painting in process on an easel. God is painted at the top of the paper, and the watery color in which God's name is sketched is pulled by gravity toward the bottom of the sheet. That color influences the other colors on the sheet—those that represent her husband, her children, and other aspects of her life.[20]

Similarly, though to a lesser degree, you are coloring and influencing your children's memories now. This is a fact that should be engraved on our hearts when we're dealing with our children. It ought to be woven through our parenting methods in discipline, encouragement, training—everywhere in the relationship between child and parent. You don't have to live as if every word, every action, might somehow damage your child, but don't underestimate the power of your words and your actions.

One woman was raised by a father who labeled her from the age of six as promiscuous. When a relative picked her up, he reminded her of what men thought of little girls who sat on their lap. If she ran and her underclothing flashed from under her dress, she was punished. From an early age, this innocent little girl's image of herself and her perception was confused. She was sharing her story as we sat together after a conference, and I then asked her to tell me about her children. Partway through describing her daughter, who was ten, she said, "She struts around and makes everyone look at her."

I stopped her immediately. "Do you realize what you just said about your daughter?"

She was defensive. "It's not the same thing. It's different than what my father did to me."

She remembered how powerful her father's words had been and the influence they had had on her life, but somehow she failed to see the effect her own words would have upon her child's memories in turn.

As you shape your children's memories, consider these principles:

1. Words are powerful.

2. We are not condemned to making the same mistakes over and over.
3. Slow down long enough to enjoy what you have while you have it.

In our success-based culture, true success is very rarely discussed. "Success" is centered around material items, body image, careers, and titles. True success, though, is what matters when you look back at the end of your life and evaluate what really mattered. It won't be your body image or the great new dress or your spotless house. It won't be the money in the bank account or the title in front of your name. It will be the people standing around you. That is the investment that will mean the most when the meaningless pursuits of life are revealed for what they are.

Adding and Contributing

Memories are not a one-time event. Therefore, you have the opportunity, at any stage of parenting, to contribute to and influence those of a son or daughter. In fact, you'll continue to add to your child's memories long after they are adults. With Melissa's wedding, I added new memories to our family album: rose petals and candles; Josh, my son-in-law, crying when his bride walked down the aisle to him; me picking them up at the airport after their honeymoon, watching them emerge from the plane hand in hand, looking very married and very happy.

And I added a new title that means the world to me: mother-in-law. My new son is a joy to us. I am now influencing his memories as a young man and young husband. My actions, and the words I say to and say about him, color and influence not only him, but his and my daughter's marriage—and one day their children. It's an amazing cycle with so much potential, but it's often overlooked.

This past summer I cheered as Leslie and Melissa walked across the stage to accept their college diplomas. Next year I will be front and center at Ryan's graduation. The children going out on their own adds new recollections: putting on a brave face the day I drove each of them to college; crying all the way home and wondering how I would make it without their lively presence; attending the first big university games; realizing how grown-up they were the first time they came home to visit. I especially remember when I first looked across the table, saw the love of my life, and realized it was just us—and how very cool that was.

I hugged Ryan's girlfriend, Jessica, when she and Ryan burst through the door in excitement one day last month. Jessica held out her finger with a ring on it, a smile breaking across her face. "I'm engaged!" It appears there are more memories ahead as I welcome one more daughter into the fold.

Life is a series of events that will one day play out as memories for our children, and the truth is, we often waste time engulfed in the past while precious moments are waiting to occur.

We have just a whisper of time to raise our children. The relationships you build with them in those 18 short years—perhaps a few more or a few less—leave a thumbprint on their hearts. Why waste that opportunity? Writer Diana Loomans reminds us of the importance of everyday moments with our children in a beautiful poem, "If I Had My Children to Raise All Over Again." She wisely suggests that if she had it to do over again, she would "finger-paint more, and point the finger less."[21]

This is wonderful advice, for you will be amazed at how quickly the memories boomerang back to you. My children are sharing theirs already. When they come home from college, we sit around the table and tell stories. They laugh and tease their dad and me. They have their special stories guaranteed to make me blush, like the time I asked one of Leslie's guy friends if he wanted to wrestle. (I was asking if he wanted to play a wrestling video game with the guys in the living room, but the words didn't come out quite right.) I still remember the astonished expression on his face.

My children delight in telling that story and laughing as they remember how embarrassed I felt and how shocked Leslie's friend was. They've even put a few twists in the story to make it better!

Up till this chapter we've focused on *your* memories. There is a distinct shift in perspective as you begin to pay attention to the memories you are creating for your own children. From this point forward, the focus is not on your past. It's on your present relationships with your current family. Let's begin that process now.

1. Describe one good family memory your child might one day share.

_____

_____

_____

_____

_____

_____

_____

_____

2. An ideal home was defined by teens as a place where you could be yourself, where you can be accepted and loved, and where the

people you love the best reside. What are your thoughts about that statement?

_____

_____

_____

_____

3. It's important that you don't overemphasize memories—worrying about every word, every small action—but what would you say is your overall home atmosphere? Is it encouraging? Is it fun?

_____

_____

_____

_____

4. Is there any one thing you wish to change?

_____

_____

_____

_____

5. What is one tangible step you and your family can implement to make that change?

_____

_____

_____

_____

6. Do you see the memories unfolding all around you? Take a moment and think about the small things your child did or said today. Write down one simple moment that will one day be a treasured memory.

_____

_____

_____

_____

7. Ask your child to tell you one thing that he or she loves about home. Listen carefully to your child's perspective. What did you learn?

_____

_____

_____

_____

Just as you have asked God to heal your memories, are you willing to ask him to make your home a special place where sweet memories will be shaped? Today may be a great time to invite him into your home.

> Father, you love my child even more than I do, don't you? You can see her heart, her talents, her sweet and tender

hopes. You see my children when they are tiny infants, full of possibilities, and when they're racing through the house, full of energy, with their imagination at full throttle. Doesn't it say that you know them so well that you've written their names on the palm of your hand, and that you have a future for them? Help me be an encourager for them. I'm glad you've given me the responsibility of shaping them. Thank you for the memories all around me and for new ones just ahead. Please come into my home today.

~

Whatever is true, whatever is noble, whatever is right, whatever is pure, whatever is lovely, whatever is admirable—if anything is excellent or praiseworthy—think about such things. Whatever you have learned or received or heard from me, or seen in me—put it into practice. And the God of peace will be with you.

—Philippians 4:8-9 NIV

If I could go back and make a list, I would like to be a parent to my children. I would be self-assured and strong and proud of who God created. I would choose to like who I am.

I would be involved and knowledgeable on all subjects, such as the needs of children and the development stages. I also would want my kids to feel safe.

My list would also include not being so afraid all the time. Afraid of what? I don't know. I think my fears stemmed from having asthma. It disabled me in so many ways.

I would like to have been the real me for my kids. Fun, creative, inventive, having fun games, and finding places to go. I would have learned about scholarships and things to get my children ready for college. I would be assured about driving and going places in the car. I would like to have been like my kids, who look forward to each new challenge.

Chapter Twelve

Making Your List

"Mom, the light from the computer is bothering me."

"Okay, son. I'll be just a moment more." I clicked on the screen to finish out the remaining hand of spades. The room was dark except for the glow of the computer screen.

Icicles draped on power lines like old chums. We were on day ten without power in our own home and had moved from our house to my in-laws' to escape the zero-degree conditions back home. My in-laws were gracious, but I felt just like Dorothy did in *The Wizard of Oz*: There's no place like home, no place like home, no place like home.

It was late, and my 17-year-old son was trying to get to sleep in the living room. I sat in front of the computer wishing I could sleep, but knowing I would toss and turn if I tried to grasp those elusive z's. I had turned off the sound and was sitting quietly.

"I'm almost through, baby. Promise."

"The light is keeping me awake. Why don't you go to bed?"

I turned. "Ryan, I said just a minute. Turn over and you won't see the light."

It quickly became a match of wills. Ryan got up on one elbow and started the verbal ping-pong, and I willingly engaged him. It was foolish, and I don't remember the exact words, but our world-class match went something like this:

Ping: Mom, I'm tired.

Pong: I'm tired too, Ry. Last night I stayed up while you and your cousins talked and laughed all night long. Can you be patient for three more minutes?

Ping: Is that over? Did you start another game?

Pong: Of course I didn't start another hand.

Ping: Mom!

Slam: Ryan!

I stood up, angry not because of the game, but because Ryan wouldn't let me sit quietly and finish. I should have graciously left the room because we were all tired and a little tense. (My son could have been more patient as well.)

I longed for my own bed, my own house, my own domain. I was ready to curl up in my brown recliner with my comfy afghan and read a book while music played in the background. Ryan was also tired. He was trying to cram his six-foot-three frame onto a short couch night after night. He longed for his own bed, his own room, a dark and quiet place where he could shut the world out and sleep.

For the next few moments my son and I wrestled verbally. Our voices were quiet, but we were both frustrated. He was tired. I felt bullied, believing that three minutes wasn't a long time to wait. I knew that the argument was unwise due to our frazzled emotions. I wanted to walk away—but not before he understood my position!

Finally Ryan made a stinging comment, and I slapped him. We both reacted with shock. I took a step back. Ryan sat up. I blushed in shame as the red handprint showed up across his cheek. But the most powerful emotion was regret. There were no words I could say to take back the physical slap. I couldn't go back and handle the situation with wisdom. It was no longer a matter of a card game or my lack of sleep or Ryan's desire for a quiet room.

~

Three children in 19 months! It definitely wasn't my plan, but you can do it if you have them in litters. When Leslie was born I thought I was the world's greatest mother. She slept only a few hours each day (she still only needs six hours of sleep a night compared to my eight), but when she was awake she was playful and observant. When I wanted to go to the store or visit friends and family, she was a joy to bring along.

I discovered I was pregnant again when Leslie was barely ten months old, and then we found out I was expecting twins. It seemed like my waistline and our family structure changed overnight. I was two months shy of my twenty-fourth birthday when Ryan and Melissa were born. The title of World's Best Mom was stripped away with the snipping of the umbilical cords.

I juggled four balls that year: love, colic, sleep deprivation, and guilt. I loved my babies. I loved the smell of their silky skin. I loved the lazy smile of my son and the fierce energy of his twin sister. I loved the blue eyes and hugs of their older sister. But caring for three children was overwhelming at times.

Melissa cried for the first few months. It normally started in the afternoon and stretched for up to four hours at a time. I consulted every expert I knew, from parenting books to our pediatrician to more experienced mothers. I tried everything. I wrapped her snugly in a blanket because one expert said she felt alone outside of the womb without her twin brother. I gave her drops prescribed by the doctor to ease stomach cramps. I eliminated foods to see if I was eating something that was causing her digestive or allergy problems. Nothing worked.

I synchronized the twins' nursing schedules so we could all get some sleep. Every three hours I nursed one baby, then the other, which left two hours to change diapers for all three children, wash a load of laundry, pick up the living room, and bathe one or more of the children, along with a host of other chores.

I was chronically sleep-deprived. Leslie had discovered how to climb over the side of her crib and would pop up beside my bed throughout the night ready to play. Between taking her back to bed and feeding the twins every three hours, I was beyond exhausted.

Then there was guilt. Leslie was less than two years old. The little girl who was used to being her momma's whole world sat at my feet with her baby doll pressed against her chest, pretending to nurse her while I switched between two hungry mouths. She carried a diaper bag into church over her tiny shoulder while Richard and I juggled a baby and carrier apiece.

Of course, that first challenging year had beautiful moments interspersed: the sweet kisses of all three of my little ones; the tiny hands kneading my face while the babies nursed.

Hitting a Wall

One night, though, all of the balls came crashing down. Richard and I owned a large farming operation, and he was outside most of every day, coming inside as often as he could to help out. I had walked the floor with Melissa for nearly five hours—a colic record. I tried not to think negative thoughts while I counted the tiles as I marched back and forth, but the truth was that I felt utterly alone and unequipped. There simply weren't enough arms and time to take care of them, us, me…

Why wouldn't she stop crying?

I looked outside and saw headlights in the distance. Richard was on his tractor. Close enough for me to know he was there, far enough away that I couldn't ask for help. I glanced at the clock. If I could hang on for just one more hour, I could pass the crying infant to him.

"Go to sleep. Go to sleep. Go to sleep, little baby," I sang softly, rubbing my thumb over her cheek. The gentle words muffled the screaming inside my brain, but not the sound from the other room of Ryan moving restlessly in his sleep. I couldn't imagine how he and Leslie slept with the racket from the wailing, ten-pound pink-wrapped package in my arms.

I glanced at the clock another time. It would soon be time to nurse—again.

Suddenly I felt something wet plop on my nose. Then another wet splash, and another. I closed my eyes as tears fell like rain. "Please, Melissa. Stop crying." Every hair on my head was standing on end. She opened her tiny mouth and wailed louder. I rushed to her crib and pushed the rail down with one hand. I took the pink bundle with my precious baby inside, planning only to set her down for two minutes so I could go out onto the back porch and take a deep breath. I gasped when she hit the mattress with a thud. Her little arms flew out, and her mouth formed an "O." For a moment the crying stopped, only to resume with greater ferocity as her fists clenched in fright and anger.

I had dropped my baby from a height of a foot or more into the baby bed.

I quickly reached for her and held her close as we both cried.

The back door opened.

"Hey, baby, I'm finally through. I got done early tonight," Richard called out.

He stopped when he saw the stricken look on my face. I placed the baby in his arms and ran out into the night.

Being Realistic with Your List

*There are only two lasting bequests we can hope to give our children.
One of these is roots, the other, wings.*

HODDING CARTER

Before I had children, I had a "good mother" list. You might have had one as well. Mine read like this:

- When I become a mother, I will play with my children.
- When I become a mother, I will not physically harm my children.
- When I become a mother, I will have a peaceful and loving home.
- When I become a mother, I will make sure they understand they are valuable as human beings.
- When I become a mother, I will never humiliate my child.

This list was born out of my own experiences and hopes. I vowed not to repeat harmful actions. I had no clue how I would make these things come about, though I was determined to try.

Dropping Melissa definitely wasn't on that list. When I heard the thud of her small body against the mattress, it was as if my greatest fears were realized. I had failed! I'll never forget how I felt as I stared up at the stars and prayed I hadn't hurt my baby. I prayed I wasn't losing control.

I understood that all was not lost, but it was a frightening moment. I could face what happened, or I could run away.

I turned around and went back into the house. I scooped up my baby, and I held her and rocked her. I shared with my husband my fears and the events leading up to dropping Melissa. That night I was forced to acknowledge one very important truth: Motherhood is downright tough—really, really tough—at times. It was great that I'd set goals, but it wasn't enough. I needed to know how to make the changes. I needed to know what to do when I failed or was close to crossing a line.

I struggled over sharing these two stories with you. It was much easier to write about my mother's transgressions than my own. But if I present myself as a perfect mother or a woman with all the answers, I miss sharing with you the parts where I learned from my mistakes. All I've ever wanted to be is a good mother. It ranks far above my desire to write or speak or succeed as a woman in any facet. I desired a safe, loving place called home, and I believe I have received that gift. But it didn't come without help and insight along the way...and even some mistakes. What did I learn?

1. Being a mom isn't always easy.
2. I can't be afraid to ask for help.
3. I need mentors.
4. I will sometimes make mistakes, and I can learn from those mistakes.

When you set parenting goals, it's vital that you be realistic. If you decide your home will be perfect, you are setting yourself up for failure. So what are *realistic* goals? Mine were to play with my children; to provide a healthy and nurturing environment; and to treat my husband with love and respect so my children would know the value of a stable, loving relationship. Another early goal was to have a home free of conflict. As my three little ones grew up, I realized this was an impossible—maybe even undesirable—goal, so I revised it to having a home where we would choose to work through conflict together.

What are your goals? What desires do you have for your family? This needs to be a proactive list. It will contain the things you choose not to do, but it will also contain those behaviors or actions you will actively work *toward* as a family.

Help Is Out There

As you make your list, and as you begin to shape the environment of your home, don't be afraid to ask for help. I read parenting books and magazines. I asked questions of women whom I trusted and whose children showed the fruit of a gentle and nurturing home.

Susan Yates, author of *And Then I Had Kids,* writes,

> Not only do our children need good role models…we need them too. Like them, we need to be exposed to other adults whom we admire. We need older Christians we can look to for encouragement in our faith. We need to know older parents who will be examples for us and who can help us with our questions about raising children.[22]

My mother-in-law is an amazing nurturer. One day I sat in her kitchen. The twins were teething and cranky. I tried to entertain them, but their little mouths hurt, and they weren't in the mood. Leslie was fidgeting and tired of listening to her siblings cry, so she was also upset. Sandra walked into the kitchen as I was struggling. She scooped up one of the twins and handed Leslie a cookie. She knew I was frustrated, but she didn't say anything. She just pitched in and gave me a hand.

I took a calculated risk. I could pretend I had it all under control, or I could be honest with this mentor in my life.

"Will it always be this hard?" I asked.

"It will get easier," she said with a smile.

"How did you do it? You had three boys in three years. Did you ever feel like you just wanted to sit and cry with them?"

She pulled up a chair and told me a story.

Her boys were all under the age of three and had the chicken pox.

She was tired and overwhelmed. She stood in the middle of her kitchen and cried like a baby.

"Then the doorbell rang, and my mother was on the front steps," she said.

Her mother brought a hot casserole and provided an extra set of hands for two days. It made all the difference.

Just knowing that another woman had once walked in my shoes comforted me. If Sandra had had bad days too, then it must be normal! Not only that, but I didn't have to do this on my own. Sometimes it was okay to ask for help when I needed it. Being a mother is both delightful and the hardest job on earth. Some days mothers need encouragement or an extra set of hands.

Positive Steps

When we find ourselves becoming the mom we don't want to be, we need to ask four questions:

1. What prompted this action or response?
2. Is there a better way to handle the situation?
3. What can I learn from this?
4. Did I resolve the situation with my child?

This brings me back to the stories I really didn't want to share.

Melissa doesn't remember the incident in the crib, because she was only four months old. But Ryan remembers the fight we had that bitter winter. It's a negative memory among the positive. We talked about that ugly night and how things escalated out of control. We were both in the wrong, but I take responsibility because I'm the adult.

In both instances I was tired and out of my comfort zone. With Melissa I needed respite. I was trying to do it all on my own. I was not only taking care of the house and kids, I was never alone. I shopped for groceries and necessities with three children in my stroller, which looked like I was pushing a small train. There were many times a well-meaning stranger would stop me in the store. "Oh, you have twins!" Then they would rouse a sleeping baby, who would then wake the other baby up, and soon I had three little ones crying. Within seconds the stranger would be long gone, and I was left standing in the middle of the store.

After the crib incident I enrolled in a program called Mother's Day Out at a local church. It was a reputable program with caring professionals who gave mothers of small children a break for a few hours a week. Moms could grocery shop or run to the mall for a couple of hours, or even do something as luxurious as to have a manicure.

But I did none of these things. Every Friday I deposited my children in capable hands and turned right around and drove home. I climbed in bed for a heavenly two-hour nap. From that time on, if I felt overwhelmed on Wednesday, I knew that on Friday I would be able to take care of my needs. It wasn't a lot of time, but it was enough.

An important key to providing a loving home is to nurture yourself along the way. It's not reasonable to expect that your goals will fall into place when you are sleep-deprived, guilt-ridden, and overwhelmed. That's what I learned when I crossed the line with Melissa. I couldn't keep juggling balls until they came crashing down on my head.

Though there were many years between the incident with baby Melissa and the teenaged Ryan, my list hadn't changed. I still desired a home where we worked through conflict and respected each other. With Ryan, I handled the original conversation with emotion rather than reason, clear direction, and purpose. I had choices. I could have finished the hand in the three minutes as I promised. I could have shut off the computer. Instead, I took the comments Ryan made and embraced them personally. I decided I was the mom and therefore I would win—at all costs. I didn't hear what he was saying, only his tone. The conversation could have been a lot different. Anything would have been better than the spat-to-nowhere in which we engaged.

Ryan may never forget that his mom crossed the line and slapped him (I sure won't), but he also remembers our talk the next morning. I apologized and acknowledged that it was the wrong way to handle the situation and that I loved him. I listened to what he had to say, and we discussed ways we could have communicated more effectively.

Ryan is a college student now, and when he talks about that incident, he is quick to say we were both in the wrong. He also says it is only a minor blip in his memory bank. He knows his mother isn't perfect. He knows my list of goals is still just as real and just as engraved on my heart.

But what if your child is already a teen and there are years of mistakes piled up like dead bones in your relationship? What if you are an older mom and your grown daughter placed this book in your hands? Our tendency is to cover up our weaknesses or defend ourselves, but acknowledging what hasn't worked gives us the opportunity for constructive change. Author Becky Tirabassi says, "If you are hiding or covering up your weaknesses and flaws from others, you are simply protecting your freedom to relapse."[23] (By "relapse," she means go back to your old behavior.)

A genuine turnaround can heal a damaged relationship at any age. How do I know that? Because when my mother began to change, I was a young adult—and it impacted me. She has continued to grow, just as I have, and the impact on me is no less powerful each time she takes another step.

It's never, ever too late to say you are sorry. It's never too late to set goals. It's never too late to learn positive methods to help you become the parent you desire to be for your child.

1. What are your goals as a mom? Be realistic.

    _____

    _____

    _____

    _____

2. Have you ever crossed the line? Think over one episode. What happened? What prompted the incident?

    _____

    _____

    _____

    _____

3. What can you learn from this incident?

    _____

    _____

    _____

    _____

4. Did you carry a pattern of behavior from your past into the situation (physical abuse, screaming, verbal abuse, and so on)? Push it out in the open where you can examine it honestly. Name it.

    _____

    _____

    _____

    _____

5. What could you have done differently? Name three alternatives.

_____

_____

_____

_____

6. Who are the parenting mentors in your life?

_____

_____

_____

_____

7. Do you ask for help when it's needed? Do you try to do it all alone? Is there a program or person who can give you a break once a week?

_____

_____

_____

_____

8. What is one thing you can do to nurture yourself so you can nurture others?

_____

_____

_____

_____

When I interviewed the teens for my book *Real Issues, Real Teens,* one thing I discovered is that no matter what a family had been through, most teens were willing to give their parents a second chance. They loved that parent—even when on the outside it appeared they had given up on the relationship. They deeply desired to connect with Mom or Dad. Your child may be snuggled in the bassinet…or spiking his hair as he gets ready to take a girl out for a date. In either instance, you are a powerful influence on his or her life. As you review your goals and even your mistakes, I hope you understand why it is important that we make realistic goals, why we continue to learn and grow, and why we will never stop in that process. I hope you will make this your prayer as you take one more step to becoming the mother you always wish you had had.

Lord, I'm not perfect, but help me adopt the attributes you have given to me so freely—grace, mercy, joy, purpose, and life! Thank you for the gift of my family. Thank you for each person in it. Thank you that you're involved with our family. Would you please help me to influence my family for good, and would you help them see your light and love inside of me as I love them with all of my heart? Thank you.

Let's not just talk about love; let's practice real love. This is the only way we'll know we're living truly, living in God's reality. It's also the way to shut down debilitating self-criticism, even when there is something to it. For God is greater than our worried hearts and knows more about us than we do ourselves.

—1 John 3:18-20

One day I was watching a show on TV. A woman was trying to get her daughter to forgive her for infidelity and other things that happened in her marriage when her daughter was younger, but the daughter wanted nothing to do with her. The mother was devastated. She was sorry for her wrongs and couldn't go on with her life because of the situation with her daughter.

I listened a little closer. The mom's name was Karen, just like mine. This thought came to me—I felt the Holy Spirit show me that I would not find 100-percent healing because I hadn't accepted responsibility—no matter what the circumstances were—for what happened when my children were young.

I messed up. It wasn't on purpose. Humans make mistakes, but subconsciously I thought that because I didn't purposely mess up as a parent, it shouldn't be counted against me. So I never really took responsibility for my actions. If I didn't take responsibility, then I was an okay person, I thought.

This thought from God opened my eyes. My daughter loved me and had forgiven me. It was time to forgive myself. But it was also time to look at my past (the way I had parented) with my children in a way it should be viewed. It was a new way of thinking.

Unpacking Your Parenting Baggage

We were driving down the highway, when Richard noticed a brown shoe in the middle of the road. Not too much farther, we saw the mate lying flattened on the asphalt. Then we saw a swath of nice clothes littered across the road. Finally we saw a battered suitcase sitting open on the shoulder.

"Somebody is going to be really disappointed when they arrive," Richard commented.

As I look back over the winding road of the past years, I see scattered here and there parenting methods I inherited that didn't fit with our family.

- I threw out "not attending my children's school events."
- I tossed out humiliation as a discipline tool.
- I eliminated rage and screaming and name-calling.

I kept a few parenting items from my childhood. I tucked it in my heart to say I'm sorry when I've done wrong, something my mom has always done. I left in my dad's laughter. I kept my mom's creative spirit.

I repacked my suitcase with new traditions and new ways of parenting. I borrowed ideas—for example, the birthday doors my sister created for my niece and nephew on their special days. I loved the idea, and ever since I've decorated my children's doors with treats and photos and balloons on their birthdays. I watched my mother and father-in-law and learned what it meant to have a close, loving family, and I integrated those same values into my goals. I prayed for guidance when I wasn't sure how to proceed. But most of all, I carefully sorted through my parenting skills and tools to find and hone those that helped my children feel secure, and that would help them learn how to be caring and responsible human beings. Unpacking my parenting baggage was not so much about giving them everything I didn't have—and much more about giving them what they truly needed.

∾

I was deep into preparations for dinner when the phone rang. My children were all coming home to spend the weekend. Their favorite meals are Mexican food, and I was in the midst of preparing chicken enchiladas, tacos, and more.

I tucked the phone under my chin and continued to cook while talking to Melissa.

"Mom, Oscar is in the backseat and he's going crazy."

Oscar was a friend she'd met her first year of college. He was a tall guy from a large urban area who had visited our home once before. It was great fun watching him ride our quarter horse, with his long legs dangling over her sides. He'd held the reins in one hand and a cell phone in the other as he reported his "wild bronc ride" (you can put a child on Annie's back because she's so gentle).

"I didn't know you had Oscar with you," I said. "How long is he stay-ing?"

"Just through the weekend. I have a couple other friends with me too."

Several of the students at Melissa's school lived hundreds of miles from their parents. Many times they'd spend long weekends alone in their dorm rooms while everyone else was gone. So it wasn't unusual for Melissa (and Ryan) to bring friends home and let them hang out with our family.

"Let me talk to him," I said. I put down what I was doing and concen-trated on the phone call. I glanced at the timer. Ten more minutes before the casserole would come out of the oven.

"What's going on, Oscar?"

"Melissa just now told me she didn't mention we were coming," he said. "Mrs. Eller, I'm sorry. She should have told you."

I laughed. "Oscar, it's fine. I'll just cook a little more. You may have to sleep on the couch or a pallet on the floor in the living room because all my kids are coming home, but it's okay."

"But I feel like I'm intruding."

"Melissa doesn't have to ask to have people come home," I replied. "She knows we're happy to have her friends here. You're always wel-come."

Oscar, Melissa, and Melissa's two other friends; Ryan and a friend from his college; and Leslie all arrived that afternoon. The house was packed and a bit messy—and we had a great time.

A New Policy to Replace the Old One

We created the open-door policy when my children were teens. My teenagers had a stricter curfew than some of their friends. We told them we thought the curfew was fair and would remain in place, but if a friend wanted to come to our home, the night could continue until their friend's curfew ended. We didn't require them to ask permission, but they did have boundaries once they arrived. They were responsible to clean up messes or any dishes used. They could have fun, but not harm each other or our home. We stocked a cabinet with snacks and soda. We stocked a shelf with games and cards, and invested in a Ping-Pong table. We kept fun and appropriate DVDs on hand.

It wasn't always convenient, but the benefit of our open-door policy was that we became a part of my children's friends' lives, and they became a part of the Eller family. One friend continues to spend holidays with us whether Ryan comes home or not. The first year he'd stayed alone in his college apartment, and when Ryan found that out, he invited him to come. We love having him, and now he feels like one of our own. Sometimes he and his girlfriend will surprise us and show up at church just to hang out with us and that's a gift. Sometimes he calls just to ask for advice or to talk. We have been blessed to be a second set of parents to many of our children's friends, and we love it.

The open-door policy is something I wanted from the beginning for our family. When I was a child, my home was not open to friends. There were times they came, but they didn't stay. They and I quickly left. Neither parent believed it was a great idea to have a noisy house full of strangers. Perhaps that was because with five kids, the house was already packed. Maybe it was my father's solitary nature. Very likely it had much to do with the chaos we were experiencing. No matter the reasons, having additional people in the house wasn't on the agenda.

Instead, I spent Friday evenings at friends' houses. I loved popping popcorn and watching movies with my friends' parents nearby. Recently I attended a couple's golden anniversary, and I felt as close to them as I did when I was a youth. That came from the hours spent under their roof watching and participating with them as a family. Their son was one of my best friends. Time in their home taught me—I watched two adults who loved each other. I listened as they teased their children playfully. I watched them correct their sons in the proper way. Even then I was gathering tools for my parenting suitcase.

What Does "Home" Mean to You?

Whenever I held my newborn baby in my arms, I used to think that what I said and did to him could have an influence not only on him but on all whom he met, not only for a day or a month or a year, but for all eternity—a very challenging and exciting thought for a mother.

ROSE KENNEDY

What makes a home? In my book for parents of teenagers, I asked some teens to share what the word "home" meant to them.

- Elizabeth, age 17, said, "I am always worried that my dad will be in a bad mood or that I haven't done everything that they asked and I will get yelled at. My parents usually fight. My home is not a safe place."

- Sarah, age 15, said, "Just being around an atmosphere of anger and arguing is hard to deal with, and it makes me angry with God for not doing something to stop it."

- Lanae, age 19, said, "My parents have always been hospitable. I really admire their hospitality. They are always ready to take someone in, whether it is for a night or for a year. They go out of their way to make others comfortable and are selfless in doing so. I would like to be selfless and hospitable, even as a college student."[24]

In these answers and many others, the definition of home through the eyes of a child had nothing to do with a house made of bricks, wood, or anything else. It wasn't about material things or perfect people. The ideal home was defined like this:

1. Home is where I feel welcome.
2. Home is a place without continual conflict.

3. Home is a place that is open to friends.

4. Home doesn't have to be perfect.

5. Home is where families play together.

As you unpack and repack your parenting baggage, redefine your idea of home. Is it a place where you can be yourself? Is it a place of acceptance and love? Is it a place of healthy interaction? Have you followed in your parents' footsteps even when the methods are destructive or ineffectual?

Many people stay trapped in harmful parenting behavior because it is familiar. In the book *Professionalizing Motherhood,* Jill Savage, founder of the organization Hearts at Home, introduces the term *home internship.* Home internship encompasses the relationship skills modeled by adults to children. If you were raised by parents who demonstrated strong relationship and parenting skills, you most likely adopted those same skills when you became a parent. If relationally destructive skills were modeled, those weaknesses may well have emerged in your parenting methods. Savage says,

> It is important that we evaluate our home internship to allow us to know both our strengths and weaknesses. Once we have identified the areas in which we are weak, we can pursue a new internship, doing whatever we can to relearn the concept in a healthy way.[25]

It's Time for Change

The following considerations are all points I had to think through in my own parenting journey. Let's walk through them together.

1. You are not limited by past parenting patterns.

2. There are helpful methods available that can positively affect your family relationships and the atmosphere of your home.

3. Your family is unique, and you and your spouse (or even your ex-spouse, if you have a cooperative relationship) can explore and implement positive methods that work for your family.

4. If you have made parenting mistakes, it is time for a 180-degree turn.

My husband is now attending college part-time. Our plan was to send our children to college, and then for Richard to return to finish his undergraduate and then his master's degree. One of his siblings remarked, "Do you realize how old you will be when you finish your degree?" My reply was, "He will turn that age whether he has a degree or not. Why not celebrate that birthday by walking across a stage and receiving a diploma?"

The traditional notion is that we are limited by circumstances, but often those limitations become excuses. We point to the past or to what we know or don't know, or to the problems and challenges in our marriage or family. We might point out the years already past and the mistakes already made.

But why not choose to learn—to read, explore, expand your mind, and grow, simply because you can? The years will pass anyway, and you will have grown rather than remaining stagnated.

When destructive parenting patterns are performed for so long that they feel "right," then they are repeated in successive generations. You might even recognize the negative results, but you persist in them because they are familiar. But as Karen O'Connor, author of *Squeeze the Moment*, points out,

> Even when we're absolutely sure we know what to do, how to do it, and where to do it, we could be wrong. Someone else might know more or have a better idea, a more interesting perspective, or a more workable plan. Consider how it might

feel to bow to that, to give up your certainty, to declare your vulnerability, to allow someone else to be right.[26]

There are helpful methods and resources available for any age group and the unique needs of a family in any stage. I have listed some of these resources in appendix A to help you repack your parenting suit-case. Don't be afraid to study these resources and meet with parent-ing mentors. You will continually sharpen your parenting skills (my children are in college and I'm still learning!). As you and I continue to be students, we unpack ineffective methods and repack our suit-case with new methods that will positively affect our relationships and create a safe place called "home" for our family.

You, or you and your spouse, will fine-tune new parenting patterns to fit your family. Not only do families have different circumstances, but there are also differences among your children. When my children were young, it took only a look to correct Leslie's behavior. She was sensitive to words, and we were careful to teach her but not tread on her gentle nature. Melissa needed us to show her how to respond by working side by side with her. She learned by doing and became frus-trated if we scolded her but didn't show her a better way. Ryan needed to simply stop whatever he was doing. He was high energy and responded to time-outs.

Your methods and consequences and rewards will be consistent, but you will also take into account the individuality of your child. These are the foundational guidelines upon which you can build your parenting methods.

What if you've already made parenting mistakes? Then hit the brakes and make a U-turn. The first step is to be honest about parent-ing methods that have done more harm than good. Acknowledge them without excuses or justification on your part, and assume responsi-bility. Ask your child for forgiveness if you have harmed him or her with words or actions. This allows you to take the lead to heal the bond between you, and it shows by example that you care as you make tangible changes.

You will explore alternative methods of training, consequences, and encouragement. Once those changes have been implemented, be consistent. Don't give up! Change is never an easy process, but over time you will learn to work together as a family and see the results.

———

Let's take a few moments as you sift through the odds and ends tucked away in your parenting suitcase. Pull them out and expose them to the light. It might be a great day to spring-clean your parenting baggage.

1. What one parenting behavior do you remember most from your childhood?

     _____

     _____

     _____

     _____

2. Take out the rest of the parenting methods you use on a regular basis. Write them down. Are they helpful or destructive?

     _____

     _____

     _____

     _____

3. What is your definition of "home"? How does it compare with the
    five points shared in this chapter (welcoming, without conflict, open
    to friends, not perfect, where families play together)? What would
    you like to do differently?

    _____

    _____

    _____

    _____

4. At this point many people offer limitations (that is, excuses): *I can't
    change because my spouse won't let me. I can't change because I like a
    perfect house. I can't change because I lose my temper no matter how
    hard I try.* Do you feel the need to list limitations? What are they?

    _____

    _____

    _____

    _____

5. Are the limitations valid, or are they excuses? Share your thoughts.

    _____

    _____

    _____

    _____

6. If they are valid limitations, what compromise can you consider to
    create a loving, safe home?

    _____

_____

_____

_____

7. List one resource you will explore in the near future to help you strengthen your parenting skills.

_____

_____

_____

_____

8. Is it possible that someone else might have a better idea or a more workable plan for you to use in parenting? Describe how it might feel to bow to that and allow someone else to teach you a brand-new way of doing things. Are you open to this?

_____

_____

_____

_____

~

We're in the homestretch. You've changed your focus from your past to that of your child's future. You live in the present and accept who you are becoming. You've unpacked and are repacking your parenting baggage. You've come a long way...and only God knows the surprises and joys that are in front of you as you continue to grow and learn. Maybe this is your prayer today:

God, I have an open suitcase just waiting for the new items to fall into place. My heart is open and willing to learn. I am ready to shape my child and influence my home as a strong, loving woman, mother, and wife. But first and foremost, I am your child. You are a safe place where I can go when I need comfort. You are my Father. I can climb up in your lap when I need you—and I need you every day. I'm so glad you wrap me in your love. Thank you for taking me this far, and thank you for what lies ahead. I know I'm not alone in this endeavor—I walk hand in hand with you.

∾

Keep your eyes on Jesus, *who both began and finished this race we're in. Study how he did it. Because he never lost sight of where he was headed—that exhilarating finish in and with God—he could put up with anything along the way: cross, shame, whatever. And now he's there, in the place of honor, right alongside God.*

—Hebrews 12:2

It's Your Turn

"Wake up, Mom! You have presents!"

It was early. We had stayed up late the night before watching a movie, and I was snuggled in bed. I stumbled out of my comfortable nest and found my way to the kitchen, where my college-aged children waited for me to open Mother's Day presents.

My hair was disheveled, and I definitely didn't look my best, but in our house presents take precedence over vanity!

Leslie, Ryan, and Melissa had pitched in to buy me a gift certificate for a day at the spa, a treat I had never enjoyed before. I oohed and aahed over the gifts. I remembered the hand plaques and colorful pictures they'd drawn when they were babies, no less precious than the store-wrapped presents now before me.

I opened Leslie's card and wiped away a tear as I read the words written at the bottom: *Now that I am becoming a woman, I want you to know you have been my example. You have taught me what a woman can be and what it means to be a mother.*

Suddenly my mind flashed back to the tiny living-and-breathing bundle placed in my arms 24 years earlier. I recalled my fear that I wouldn't or couldn't be what she needed. I smiled at my beautiful daughter through my tears, and she patted me on the shoulder. "Oh, Mom—don't cry. It's just a card," she said, reaching down to give me a hug.

She might not ever understand, but it was far more than a card to me. Her words expressed all I had ever hoped for. No matter what I do in life, my primary calling has been to shape and impact the lives of Leslie, Melissa, and Ryan. The word *mother* is sacred to me.

At this stage of my children's lives, I see that influence emerging. Leslie and Melissa served as camp counselors in another state for a summer. "Oh my goodness, Mom. You would not believe how many times I talked to my kids and heard your words coming out of my mouth," Melissa said after returning.

"I think I saw what kind of mother I might be one day," Leslie added with a grin.

My son is a young man, but the playfulness we saw in him when he was a little boy has emerged all over again. Watching him and his fiancée is much like watching two puppies at play. One day they came to visit for an afternoon and brought her little nephew with them. When they stepped out of the car, he was between them. Ryan and his fiancée held his hands and swung him in the air as he shrieked in delight.

Just like Richard and I used to do with Ryan.

I can see the people they have become and the parents they will be one day. I am already praying for Melissa and Josh. In fact, I'm praying for all my children and their future spouses. I pray for their relationships and for the children they will one day bring into the world.

～

Our children are presented to us undeveloped. Life will shape them. Experiences will direct and mark them. Outside influences will try to steal them away at times. They will grow up with their own wills and personalities. Through it all, your fingerprints will be gently impressed on their lives.

What impressions will you leave on the heart of your child? What will your child glean from their growing up years and one day share with the next generation? You have begun a great journey. The past is behind you, and in front of you is a brand-new day. What will you do with it?

It's your turn now to create a legacy.

Additional Resources

About Forming Your Spiritual Life:

Prayerwalk: Becoming a Woman of Prayer, Strength, and Discipline, by Janet Holm McHenry. WaterBrook Press.

Legacy of Prayer: A Spiritual Trust Fund for the Generations, by Jennifer Kennedy Dean. New Hope Publishers.

The Burning Heart Contract, by Becky Tirabassi. Integrity.

The Power of a Praying® Woman, by Stormie Omartian. Harvest House Publishers.

The Power of a Praying® Parent, by Stormie Omartian. Harvest House Publishers.

Sharing His Secrets, by Vickey Banks. Multnomah Publishers.

About Setting Boundaries:

Boundaries Face to Face: How to Have That Difficult Conversation You've Been Avoiding, by Henry Cloud and John Townsend. Zondervan.

About Women Who Overcame Difficult Life Situations:

The Groovy Chicks' Roadtrip to Peace, by Dena Dyer and Laurie Copeland. Life Journey.

God Allows U-Turns—A Woman's Journey: True Stories of Hope and Healing, by Allison Bottke. Barbour Publishing.

She's Come Undone: Replacing the Lies Women Believe with God's Truth, by Allison Bottke, Tracie Peterson, and Dianne O'Brian. Bethany House.

Deceived by Shame, Desired by God, by Cynthia Spell Humbert. NavPress Publishing.

About Parenting:

And Then I Had Kids, by Susan Alexander Yates. Baker Books.

Aaron's Way: The Journey of a Strong-Willed Child, by Kendra Smiley. Moody Publishers.

High-Wire Mom, by Kendra Smiley. Moody Publishers.

Professionalizing Motherhood, by Jill Savage. Zondervan.

Don't Make Me Count to Three: A Mom's Look at Heart-Oriented Discipline, by Ginger Plowman. Shepherd Press.

Angry Teens and the Parents Who Love Them, by Sandy J. Austin. Beacon Hill Press.

Real Issues, Real Teens: What Every Parent Needs to Know, by T. Suzanne Eller. Life Journey.

About Healing:

When You Hurt and When He Heals, by Jennifer Kennedy Dean. Moody Publishers.

After the Locusts: Restoring Ruined Dreams, Reclaiming Wasted Years, by Jan Coleman. Broadman and Holman.

Making Peace with Your Past, by H. Norman Wright. Revell.

Mending Your Heart in a Broken World, by Patsy Clairmont. Warner Faith.

Redeeming the Past, by David A. Seamands. Victor Books.

Total Forgiveness, by R.T. Kendall. Charisma House.

The Prayer of Revenge, by Doug Schmidt. Cook Communications.

About Sexual Abuse:

Shelter from the Storm: Hope for Survivors of Sexual Abuse, by Cynthia Kubetin and James Mallory. Lifeway Press.

Leader's Guide

Message for Facilitators

As you meet with women to explore healing, you may feel ill-equipped in the beginning. You are not being asked to fix anyone, but to facilitate discussions and share tools so the Holy Spirit might help people and heal them according to his timing.

In one of his books, Dr. Les Parrott III shared the results of a four-year study in regard to the three qualities that contribute to successful groups. They are warmth, knowing that people are genuine, and empathy. He went on to say that the best conditions for growth occur when the group members…

1. feel they are accepted unconditionally
2. feel they are with someone who is trustworthy
3. feel they are understood

As you begin the meetings, the women may not share openly. They may wait to see if you and others are truly listening before they tell their story. One way to let someone know you are listening is to ask reflective questions and then to clarify their response.

I'd like to share three examples that might help explain this better.

Example #1

Woman: I don't think I can forgive my mom.

Facilitator: Are you saying you can't do it on your own? *(Reflective question.)*

Woman: Yes. I've tried. It's impossible. *(Honest answer.)*

Facilitator: It sounds like you are saying you would be willing to forgive if you knew how. Is that what I'm hearing? *(Clarifying question.)*

Woman: If I thought it was possible, then I'd definitely be willing to try again. (*Hopeful response.*)

Active listening helped the facilitator to discover not only what was said, but what was unspoken. The questions confirmed the woman's desire for healing and affirmed it was possible with help and practical resources. Reflective questions allow a person to discover answers on their own.

Example #2

Woman: I don't think I can forgive my mom.

Facilitator: The Bible says we should forgive. We can't find healing until that step is taken. *(Blanket statement. Where can the conversation go now?)*

Woman: That's what makes this so hard. God has forgiven me, but I can't forgive my mother. *(Guilt)*

Facilitator: Taking that step is key to your healing. Are you ready to do it today? *(Facilitator isn't listening.)*

Woman: I don't feel like I can.

Here, the facilitator stated what the woman already knew. She is there because she knows forgiving is healthy, but she's not sure where to begin. When you state the obvious, you miss an opportunity for participants to delve deeper into the topic or into their feelings. It also opens the door for judgment. There was also pressure to make a decision. Remember, this isn't a race. It's the beginning of a lifelong journey for each woman. You don't have to see immediate results in a woman's life in order for progress to occur.

Example #3

Woman: I don't think I can forgive my mom.

Facilitator: Are you saying you believe you can't do it on your own?

Woman: I've tried. It's impossible.

Woman #2: I used to struggle with it too, but God helped me to forgive. Maybe you haven't tried hard enough.

Facilitator: What I hear you *(woman #2)* saying is that God helped you. That's awesome *(affirmation)*. But trying hard without knowing what to do or where to turn can be frustrating. What I think I hear her *(turning to woman #1)* saying is that she wants to forgive, but would like to know how. Is that correct?

Woman #1: If I knew the next step to take, I'd definitely try again.

In this example, active listening kept the group discussion on track. Your goal isn't to have an inflexible atmosphere, but you do want to allow each woman to speak and then redirect conversation if it becomes unhelpful. The job of facilitating is much like being a traffic director. Sometimes you gently hold up the stop sign while you guide conversation into a more productive lane. It's not overwhelming or embarrassing anyone, but rather affirming and loving women as you smooth the progress of the discussion.

A Safe Place

How do you make small groups a safe place? Make the room warm and inviting. There is nothing worse than a bare Sunday-school classroom, for instance. Jazz it up with pretty flowers and unscented candles. Create a circle where women can sit close and see each other. Ask them to bring their favorite finger foods. Bring chocolate! Create an atmosphere that is comfortable and inviting.

Don't be afraid to have fun and form friendships. Laughter and connection with other women can be an important part of healing.

Confidentiality is crucial. Respect for one another is also a key factor. There are no wrong answers, only a diversity of experiences and perspectives.

Group Size

Individual groups should be no larger than eight to ten women. This allows intimacy within the group and gives everyone a chance to share if they wish.

Where to Begin

Each week, allow the members time to choose something to eat and drink and to mingle for a few minutes. Begin with a brief icebreaker. This allows the meeting to begin on a fun note. Previously, you'll have assigned the women to read one chapter and work through the personal questions at the end of each chapter. You'll begin with one of those questions. Allow them to volunteer their information. Some women won't respond right away but will join in later as they feel comfortable.

Most of the personal (and therefore most difficult) exploration will have already taken place as the women read the book at home. The purpose of the group is encouragement, friendship, and additional enlightenment as you work together.

Going Deeper

When I teach the college-age discipleship class at my local church, I often tell them to put on their gear because we're going deep. No snorkeling—we are scuba diving today! The questions for each small-group session are designed to take the women deeper into the topic of that week's chapter.

They may struggle during these deeper questions. I was teaching a workshop at a conference, and a woman left the room crying. I asked my helper to find her and comfort her while I remained focused on the rest of the session. Afterward I found her, and we talked over what had occurred. She had hit an emotional roadblock and was angry and embarrassed. I assured her she was peeling back a layer of pain and I wasn't afraid of that pain, nor was God. Exposing it was a key to allowing God to heal the hurt. So it's important you have someone you trust to help you just in case a woman needs a friend during a meeting.

The next step is to discuss a practical tool or resource each woman can use or explore on the topic. Last, end the meeting with prayer. It is a great time to connect with each other.

I'm asking God to help, encourage, and heal you and everyone who participates in these meetings. He knows by name every woman who will walk through the door. He loves her. He's grieving over her hurt, and he will celebrate as she grows as a woman and mother.

He also knows you. Ask him to take you on a personal adventure as you facilitate this group. When you see God bringing about subtle changes in the hearts of other women, you are enjoying an opportunity to watch him perform miracles. When I speak to or teach others, I learn more about myself and more about God every time.

Week One

Introductory Meeting

Provide finger foods and coffee and tea (you can ask your helper to invite others to bring snacks to the next meeting).

Icebreaker: Have everyone sit in a circle. Give every woman in the room an M&M. Go around the circle and ask each person to share her name and also to share one thing, based on the color of their M&M:

- *yellow*—something nice about yourself
- *green*—the most relaxing place in your home

- *red*—your most embarrassing moment
- *blue*—your best day ever
- *brown*—your favorite food
- *black*—one thing you are afraid of doing*

The introductory meeting has two purposes. The first is to get to know each other and to experience the comfort of joining other women in a safe environment. The second is to introduce the format for the next 13 sessions. Hand out copies of the book and share the following instructions:

1. Read one chapter per week.
2. Don't read ahead. (*Reading* something is different than *processing* it. They might want to read through the chapter once, put it aside, and then pick it up a day later and read it again.)
3. Answer the questions at the end of each chapter. Be real.
4. One of the questions will be discussed at the beginning of the next meeting (don't share in advance which question), as well as additional questions and practical helps.

Share the following guidelines for mutual relationships:

1. We will respect each other. (Every person is at a different place in her journey.)
2. We will encourage one another.
3. We will honor each other. (What is shared in the group meeting is confidential.)
4. We will have fun and make new friends during this process.
5. We will pray for each other.

---

* You may have to do a little searching to find black M&Ms. Or simply substitute a different multicolored candy.

Join hands and pray for one another. Invite God to be a part of the process. Dismiss.

Shattered Legacies (Chapter 1)

Icebreaker: Take a ball of yarn and select a person to hold one end and wrap it around their wrist. They will throw the yarn to someone else in the room and say something positive about that person. The person who catches it then does the same. After everyone has caught the yarn, they will all be connected. Have them keep the yarn on their wrists for the moment.

Chapter question: Did you recognize repeated patterns of dysfunction in your family tree? What were they?

Going deeper:

1. You are connected to your friend or acquaintance in this group by the sincere compliment she shared with you. But in a way you are also connected to generational patterns passed down to you. At any point, these patterns can be broken. What is one generational pattern you would like to break for your child? (Ask the women to break the yarn and take it from their wrist after they answer the question.)

2. Did you see similarities in Suzanne's and her mother's childhood stories? As you read about them, what were your thoughts?

3. How do you feel about the possibility of growing as a person and as a mother?

Application: Ask the women to take their length of yarn home and put it in a visible place as a reminder of the legacies handed from generation to generation. Remind them that the legacies that connect us can be positive or negative.

Prayer: Ask the women to write the name of their children on a piece of paper and then find a private place to pray and ask God to break the cycle with their children.

Broken Mirrors (Chapter 2)

Icebreaker: Have each person write down one thing about herself that most people might not know (can wiggle nose, ran a marathon, used to be shy, and so on) and place it in a deflated balloon. Have them blow up the balloon and toss it into the middle of the circle. Each person will choose a balloon, pop it, and pull out the piece of paper—and the whole group will try to guess the identity of the one who wrote on it.

Chapter question: If your past is only one small ingredient of who you are, then describe the other ingredients.

Going deeper:

1. What were your thoughts on the concept of a looking-glass self?

2. Psalm 139:13-15 describes a very different looking-glass self. Though you may struggle to see yourself that way, God has viewed you like that from the very beginning. Why is it a challenge to see ourselves the way God does?

3. How do you believe a parent shapes a child's looking-glass self?

4. Go around the circle and share a couple of positive (and meaningful) words that describe your child.

Application: Have a postcard with each woman's name printed artistically on one side. Place the cards around the room with a pen for each.

Ask the women to take a few moments and to write a note of encouragement to each person whose name is on the card. If that person inspires them, ask them to write that on the card. If someone is beautiful or gracious, ask them to share that. At the end of the night, ask each woman to take their card with them and read it in private.

Ask them to consider writing a similar note of encouragement for their child or children, and spouse if they're married.

Prayer: Join together and pray for each other. Ask God to reveal each woman's beauty to her through his grace.

Becoming Willing to Forgive (Chapter 3)

Icebreaker: Have the group stand close together. Tell them to reach out their arms so all their hands are jumbled together. Tell them to grab one hand in each of their hands, but not the hands of the people on either side of them.

Now they are a human knot and must use teamwork to untangle themselves into one large figure without letting go of their hands. This is a fun icebreaker, but it might take some work to untangle the mess of hands and arms. Sometimes people have to twist and turn and even pose in uncomfortable positions to work out of the knot. There are four possible solutions to the knot:

1. One large circle with people facing either direction.
2. Two interlocking circles.
3. A figure eight.
4. A circle within a circle.

Chapter question: This week you wrote down the real impact of anger, bitterness, or resentment from the past on you or your immediate family (children, or children and spouse). Can you share what you wrote?

Going deeper:

1. Nurture is normally a positive word. We nurture our children. We nurture kittens and plants and people. But what does it mean to nurture our anger?

2. Suzanne said she chose to forgive her father. Is forgiveness really a choice?

3. At this point, all that is asked of each of you is to be willing to forgive. What is the difference between being willing to forgive and forgiving?

4. At the beginning of tonight's meeting, you were tied in a human knot. What helped you find your way out? Do you sometimes need help to find your way out of bitterness or anger?

Application: Have you ever learned something new or different? Did it seem impossible in the beginning (making a pie from scratch, driving, speaking in front of a group)? Learning new things takes instruction. It takes effort. It takes time. Forgiving sometimes feels like untangling the human knot. It's a process, and it might take time and the encouragement of others. The outcome is resolution! Are you willing to be patient with yourself and with the process?

Prayer: Have them form groups of two or three. In those small groups, ask them to pray for each other and ask God to help with this stage of the healing journey.

<hr>

Week Five
"It's Hard to Forgive" (Chapter 4)

Icebreaker: Have each woman finish this sentence: "If I could learn how to do one new thing [sing, sew, fly, dance, and so on], it would be

_____, because _____."

Chapter question: Do you ever feel you need to make the people in your past pay for their actions? (Invite the women to share an example, but only if they wish.)

Going deeper:

1. One of the quotes in this chapter reads, "Total forgiveness...must take place in the heart. If I have a genuine heart-experience, I will not be devastated if there is no reconciliation." Why is forgiving still important even if there is no reconciliation?

2. There were three reasons listed describing why it is hard to forgive. Did any of the three apply to you?

3. What does it mean to you personally to be an accountant of wrongs? What is the effect of that upon current relationships (with your spouse, children, co-workers, or friends)?

4. How can the memories of your past be used in a positive manner? Have you ever thought about your past in this light before? Let's talk about that.

Application: Last week we talked about willingness to forgive. This week we've discussed why it is hard to forgive. In our icebreaker, we talked about new skills we'd love to develop in our lives. Learning to forgive is also a new skill, one that offers life-changing rewards to you and your family. Write on a piece of paper three benefits for you, your family, or both if you choose to learn how to forgive.

Prayer: Pray for each other in a circle. Ask God to bring joy to each woman as she explores this painful subject. Thank God for each woman's courage and ask God to give her peace, strength, and joy as she goes through her week.

A Second Helping of
"It's Hard to Forgive" (Chapter 5)

Icebreaker: Bring a blank canvas, paintbrushes, and acrylic paints to class. As each woman enters the room, ask her to paint her favorite color on the canvas. Explain that this is an abstract painting and there are no rules. It's an expression of color and connection.

Chapter question: Have you devoted energy to unforgiveness that you are now willing to devote to greater passions?

Going deeper:

1. Have you ever considered that, if you don't forgive or deal with the past, your offender continues to abuse you and your family? What are your thoughts?

2. What one relational tool can we give our children to help them have strong, healthy relationships now and in the future?

3. Should another person's inability to say they are sorry keep you from wholeness? Why or why not?

4. There were three reasons why it's hard to forgive listed in this chapter. Did any of the three apply to you?

Application: (Have the women study the painting.) This painting is an expression of the women in the class. The beautiful colors bleed into each other, wash over each other, complement each other. Some of the stronger shades change other colors to brand-new hues.

In our families, we all bring our own colors to the picture. Strong harsh colors such as bitterness or rage might overpower the gentler colors. Sometimes our colors bleed into other colors, producing something even more beautiful, maybe even unexpected. Each color, every color, affects the colors around it. The new colors that are emerging, such as compassion, joy, and healing, will spread out over your family's canvas, producing a new portrait.

Assignment: This week you will ask the women to do a home assignment. They are to buy a canvas and paint an abstract picture with their child. They will paint their child in the colors that reflect the best of that child's personality. The child is free to use colors to paint however he or she wishes. Note the colors the child chooses. Note the freedom and fun he or she brings to the project while playing with color and shading and texture. As they and their child paint together, ask the women to reflect on how the colors in her life impact the child at her side.

Prayer: Have the women gather around the easel. Holding hands, pray for each other and ask God to bring healing colors into each person, each marriage, and each family.

WEEK SEVEN

The Power of Perspective (Chapter 6)

Icebreaker: If you were to be executed and were offered a last meal, what would you choose?

Chapter question: How many of you have used the excuse "That's just the way I am"? Let's talk about that. How does using this excuse keep us from growing?

Going deeper:

1. Have you stopped to count your miracles lately? Name one.

2. Is it possible to broaden your perspective if you are a pessimist? How?

3. Each of us is very different in temperament and personality. If the world was comprised of only optimists, there would be great enthusiasm, but perhaps not as much

accomplished. What are the struggles when diverse temperaments are all under one roof?

4. How does your perspective affect your outlook? Your family? Your response to others?

Application: Write down five good things in your life. They can be large or small or a mixture of both. Carry this with you throughout the week. If you get stressed, take it out and reflect and refocus on those good things.

Prayer: This will be a "popcorn" prayer session that you will begin. Ask each woman, as they are comfortable, to thank God for one good thing in her life. There may be silence as the women contemplate what they want to say, but be patient. After a few moments close out the prayer by thanking God for each of the women in the room.

WEEK EIGHT
Setting Boundaries (Chapter 7)

Icebreaker: By this point everyone should be comfortable with each other enough to play this game. Prepare slips of paper with sequential numbers on them, one number on each slip. Give a number to each woman and then blindfold all of them. They must line up in order without talking.

Chapter question: In regard to a still-dysfunctional loved one, are you prepared for this person to be angry or react when you set boundaries? Name one reason why you love that person enough to let them be angry.

Going deeper:

1. Suzanne said there's a difference between setting reasonable boundaries and rigid rules. What is the difference, and why it is important to know the difference?

2. Is it difficult for you to set boundaries because of your background?

3. What were your thoughts when Suzanne described boundaries as invitations to share your needs with others?

4. Which of the guidelines do you need to implement with your current family? How can that strengthen your relationships?

Application: When you were blindfolded earlier, describe the emotions you felt as you tried to find your place in line.

Many times when dysfunction continues past childhood, an adult child will feel out of place in her family. She is not a child, but she's not treated like a grown-up. A lack of clear communication makes it difficult to establish a healthy relationship. Setting boundaries is one way you can begin to assert your adult standing with a dysfunctional parent or loved one.

Write down two boundaries that need to be communicated this week.

Prayer: Ask the women to find a partner and pray together for wisdom and compassion as they share those boundaries at the appropriate time.

Week Nine
Breaking Down Walls (Chapter 8)

Icebreaker: Draw a circle on the ground two feet in diameter. Call this the "island." The entire group must figure out a way to stay on the island together for two minutes.

Chapter question: What is the difference between setting boundaries and tearing down walls? Describe how boundaries empower relationships, while walls divide.

Going deeper:

1. What benefits do we gain when we tear down walls?

2. Is tearing down walls a process? How important is it to be patient with ourselves through the process?

3. At the beginning of class, the icebreaker was fun, but it took a lot of energy to stay inside the circle. How much energy does it take to keep personal walls up in your life?

4. What is one tool we've studied (in the past several weeks) that is helping you to chip away at the walls in your life? Give an example.

Application: Ask each woman to write one personal desire on a postcard (for example, "I want to laugh more"; "I want to take more risks"; "I want to stop losing my temper so much"). This is a vulnerable moment—it's chipping away at the wall. Remain in the circle, but have the women face each other in pairs and share their written need with their partner and pray for each other. Then they will carefully destroy the postcards, assuring each other they will honor their trust and keep in confidence what was shared.

Prayer: Create a healthy wall as women link together in a circle to pray for each other and thank God for the progress in their journey.

WEEK TEN

Becoming a Risk-Taker (Chapter 9)

Icebreaker: The group sits in a circle. Each person is given a sheet of paper and pen or pencil. The leader asks everyone to relax for a few minutes and take two deep breaths. They are to think about a person who knows them very well—a spouse, a sibling, a friend—someone they can call a best friend. With a clear picture of that person in their mind, have them take the piece of paper and write down how that person would introduce them.

These are some possibilities:

- "_____ is the kind of person who likes __

   _____."

- "Someday, _____ would like to _____

   _____."

- "_____ is passionate about _____

   _____."

- "_____ is my best friend because _____

   _____."

Chapter question: What is your reaction to the idea of F.E.A.R. (false evidence appearing real)?

Going deeper:

1. Give an example of risky behavior versus taking a calculated risk.

2. What are the "what ifs" that keep you from taking calculated risks?

3. How important is taking risks in your journey to healing? What if your attempts aren't 100-percent successful in the eyes of others?

4. List one positive motivation for taking risks (personal growth, learn new things, and so on).

Application: Suzanne's personal mission statement was "Do it afraid." Take ten minutes and consider your own mission statement. Write it in bold colors on a postcard and place it where you can see it every day.

Prayer: Get alone and consider who you are in the eyes of your best friend, God. Ask him to help you as you become a risk-taker.

Letting Go (Chapter 10)

Icebreaker: Discuss "firsts" in your life. (Some examples are first kiss; first baby; first job; first boyfriend; first new home.) Describe a "first" and how it impacted you.

Chapter question: Describe a transformation that has taken place in your once dysfunctional family since you were a child. (Not everyone will be able to participate in this, as some will have parents who are still dysfunctional.)

Going deeper:

1. Suzanne was surprised she saw her parent through the eyes of a "half-child / half-woman." What do you think she meant? What does this mean to you personally?

2. Why is letting go important even if your parent is deceased?

3. What does the word *relinquishment* mean to you?

4. What are the needs of your parent? What is he or she searching for? (Explain to the women they may not have the power to fulfill those needs, especially in the case of still-dysfunctional parents.) What do you receive by recognizing the needs of others?

Application: Ask the women to share one thing they wish to let go at this point. Letting go may be a "first" for some of the women. If so, it is a monumental moment and should be celebrated.

Prayer: Take the women to a larger room, perhaps a sanctuary. Dim the lighting for privacy and play gentle music (again, to grant each person privacy). Ask the women to find an alone place where they can talk to God. Let them know this is a safe place to leave behind the things that keep them trapped in the past. Remind them that they may try to pick them back up, but that there is always a safe place (with God). They may have to let them go many times, until one day they have no desire to pick them back up.

Week Twelve

Your Children's Memories (Chapter 11)

Icebreaker: Have the women all close their eyes and take turns describing what the person next to them is wearing from head to toe (color of shoes, pants or skirt, shirt, dress, jewelry). Afterward they are to look at the person next to them to see how close they were in their answers. The person with the most correct answers wins a small prize.

Chapter question: Did your child share one thing he or she loves about home? What did you learn from their response?

Going deeper:

1. What are your thoughts about this statement? "We often focus on our past memories, but fail to realize we are making our children's memories now."

2. What is your definition of an ideal home environment? What is your child's definition?

3. Share one thing your child did or said recently that will one day be a treasured memory.

4. Memories are not a one-time event. How optimistic are you when you realize you have many memory-shaping opportunities ahead?

Application: Share as a group about practical, fun, or everyday things (eating together, birthday doors, fun things to do with children that require little money) that make a home a nice place to be. Creative or practical ideas may emerge that become new traditions for others.

Prayer: Invite God into the group and into each home. Pray for new beginnings.

Making Your List (Chapter 12)

Icebreaker: Brainstorm and come up with a group top-ten list of the most fun things to do on a rainy day.

Chapter question: Who are the parenting mentors in your life?

Going deeper:

1. Suzanne described a time when her daughter was experiencing colic and she felt overwhelmed. Have you ever felt unequipped as a mother? (The women may share examples if they wish.)

2. What are practical resources you've used to sharpen your parenting skills?

3. How important is it to have a mentor if you did not have a positive parenting example in your own childhood?

4. Did you experience any lightbulb moments as you read this chapter? Share one and how it impacted you.

Application: Brainstorm as a group to find creative ways women can nurture themselves as a woman and mother. Bring fun and creative postcards to class. Have the women write down one nurturing tip or activity on the card (take a bubble bath while my husband or someone else watches the children, get a manicure, have lunch with a friend). Have them address it to themselves and give it to you. Throughout the next week, drop the postcards in the mail. Tell the women that when it shows up in their mailbox, it's a reminder of their nurturing appointment.

Prayer: We often make lists of groceries and appointments, but today take time alone with God and list your hopes as a mother with him. Give that list to him.

Unpacking Your Parenting Baggage
(Chapter 13)

Icebreaker: Set up two teams. Each team will receive one pair of new garden gloves and one pack of gum (five pieces per pack). On "go," the first person in each team is to put on the garden gloves, open the pack of gum, pull out a piece, unwrap it, put it in her mouth, and then pass the gloves and package to the next person. The first team to unpack all the gum wins.

Chapter question: What is your definition of home? How does it compare with the five points shared in this chapter (welcoming; without conflict; open to friends; not perfect; where families play together)? What would you like to do differently?

Going deeper:

1. How difficult was it to unpackage the gum with the gloves on? How often do old parenting methods frustrate you or others in your home?

2. If you shared something you would like to do differently, what is one step you can take to make that change?

3. What is one parenting method you would like to *keep* in your parenting suitcase?

4. Jill Savage of the Hearts at Home organization uses the term *home internship.* She says it is important to know both your strengths and weaknesses. Name one strength and one weakness.

5. Is it possible to change the way you parent your child? What is one helpful resource to help you begin that process?

6. This is our last week. What one thing do you need from the group as you continue on in your personal journey (prayer, encouragement, a hug, chocolate!)?

Application: Make a list—not a wish list, but a prayer list—for your home. Describe the attributes you and your family desire to have in your home and family.

Prayer: Ask the women to tuck this list in a devotional book or their Bible—somewhere they'll see on a daily basis. Ask them to pray over their home, children, and marriage daily.

It's Your Turn

My hope for your small group is that friendships will have been formed and strengthened over the past several weeks. Ending a session is never easy; however, it is a celebration. It's not the end of the process. It's just begun.

Though the meetings have ended, encouragement will continue as the women stay connected as friends. There is simply something beautiful about girlfriends who aren't afraid to get real about their lives and who celebrate with each other as they overcome challenges.

Notes

1. Erwin R. McManus, *Uprising* (Nashville, TN: Nelson, 2003), pp. 137, 139.
2. Jennifer Kennedy Dean, *When You Hurt and When He Heals* (Chicago: Moody Publishers, 2004), p. 86.
3. David Seamands, *Healing for Damaged Emotions* (Colorado Springs, CO: Chariot Victor, 1981), p. 11.
4. R.T. Kendall, *Total Forgiveness* (Lake Mary, FL: Charisma House, 2002), p. 3.
5. Kendall, p. 29.
6. Adapted from T. Suzanne Eller, "Second Chances," *Christian Parenting Today,* Summer, 2005, p. 39.
7. Cynthia Kubetin and James Mallory, *Shelter from the Storm* (Nashville, TN: LifeWay Press, 1995), p. 162.
8. Seamands, as quoted at http://en.thinkexist.com/quotes/david_seamands/.
9. Ron Luce, *Battle Cry* (Colorado Springs, CO: Cook Communications, 2005), p. 59.
10. "All that Glitters Is Not Gold," in *The Day I Met God,* Lori Trice, Jim and Karen Covell, and Victorya Michaels Rogers, eds. (Sisters, OR: Multnomah, 2001), p. 140.
11. Doug Schmidt, *The Prayer of Revenge* (Colorado Springs, CO: Cook, Next Gen, 2003), p. 33.
12. Cecil Murphey, *Committed, but Flawed* (Chattanooga,TN: AMG, 2004), p. 89.
13. Stormie Omartian, in Ginger Kolbaba, "The Power of Prayer," *Today's Christian Woman,* July/August 2002.
14. See the book of Ruth, chapters 1 and 2.
15. Janet Congo, *The Self-Confident Woman* (Colorado Springs, CO: Life Journey, 2003), p. 115.
16. Congo, p. 117.
17. McManus, p. 89.
18. See the book of Matthew, chapter 14.
19. Dean, p. 115.
20. Kendra Smiley, *High-Wire Mom* (Chicago: Moody Publishers), p. 26.
21. From Diana Loomans, "If I Had My Child to Raise All Over Again," as found in the book *100 Ways to Build Self-Esteem and Teach Values* (Tiburon, CA: HJ Kramer, Inc., 2003).

22. Susan Yates, *And Then I Had Kids* (Grand Rapids, MI: Baker Books), p. 147.

23. Becky Tirabassi, *The Burning Heart Contract* (Brentwood, TN: Integrity, 2005), p. 51.

24. T. Suzanne Eller, *Real Issues, Real Teens: What Every Parent Needs to Know* (Colorado Springs, CO: Life Journey, 2004), pp. 163-164, 168-169.

25. Jill Savage, *Professionalizing Motherhood* (Grand Rapids, MI: Zondervan, 2001), p. 141.

26. Karen O'Connor, *Squeeze the Moment* (Colorado Springs, CO: Waterbrook, 1999), p. 18.

27. Dr. Les Parrott III, *Helping the Struggling Adolescent* (Grand Rapids, MI: Harper Collins and Zondervan, 2000), pp. 29, 32. Parrott is citing *Characteristics of Effective Helping*, a 1967 study by Carl Rogers.

About the Author

In addition to *The Mom I Want to Be,* T. Suzanne Eller has authored *Real Teens, Real Stories, Real Life* and *Real Issues, Real Teens: What Every Parent Needs to Know.* She is also an international speaker to teens, women, and families. To contact Suzanne to speak to your ministry or organization, please e-mail her at tseller@daretobelieve.org.

T. Suzanne Eller
c/o Dare To Believe
2071 Amelia Court
Tahlequah, OK 74464
www.daretobelieve.org

Hearts at Home®

The Hearts at Home organization is committed to meeting the needs of women in the profession of motherhood. Founded in 1993, Hearts at Home offers a variety of resources and events to assist women in their jobs as wives and mothers.

In addition to this book and others, our resources include the *Hearts at Home* magazine, the *Hearts at Home* online newsletter, and the Hearts at Home Web site. Additionally, Hearts at Home events make a great getaway for individuals, moms' groups, or for that special friend, sister, or sister-in-law. The regional conferences, attended by more than 10,000 women each year, provide a unique, affordable, and highly encouraging weekend for the woman who wants to grow as a mother.

Hearts at Home
1509 N Clinton Blvd
Bloomington, Illinois 61701-1813
Phone: (309) 888-MOMS
Fax: (309) 888-4525
E-mail: hearts@hearts-at-home.org
Web site: www.hearts-at-home.org

Harvest House
Helps Moms!

Got Teens?: Time-Tested Answers for Mom of Teens and Tweens
by Jill Savage and Pam Farrel

Jill Savage, founder of Hearts at Home Ministries, and Pam Farrel, cofounder of Masterful Living Ministries, help you with practical, biblical tools to

- identify and develop strengths
- make choices over what kids can do, and with who
- teach manners, compassion, and social responsibility
- guide relationships with the opposite sex
- turn around destructive behavior and or bad habits

In this fresh look at parenting, moms will discover how to better face the hardest and most rewarding job of their lives.

MORE GREAT RESOURCES FOR MOMS

10-Minute Time Outs for Moms
by Grace Fox

Insightful devotions from author and mother Grace Fox empower you to maintain a vital connection with God. Inspiring stories, Scripture-based prayers, and practical guidance will give you strength for your spiritual journey and daily life.

Keep It Simple for Moms on the Go
by Emilie Barnes

How can you cross everything off your "to do" list? By keeping it simple. Bestselling author Emilie Barnes reveals creative ways moms can simplify their lives, including easy decorating tips, motherly wisdom, and spiritual insights.

HARVEST HOUSE
PUBLISHERS

Resources for Life Change
from Harvest House Publishers

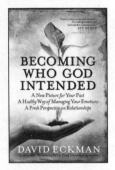

Becoming Who God Intended
by David Eckman

Whether you realize it or not, your imagination is filled with *pictures* of reality. The Bible indicates these pictures reveal your true "heart beliefs"—the beliefs that actually shape your everyday feelings and reactions to family, friends, and others, to life's circumstances, and to God.

David Eckman compassionately shows you how to allow God's Spirit to build new, *biblical* pictures in your heart and imagination. As you do this, you will be able to accept God's acceptance of you in Christ, break free from negative emotions and habitual sin...and finally experience the life God the Father has always intended for you.

> "I strongly urge you to get *Becoming Who God Intended* and put it to work in your life."
>
> **Josh McDowell**

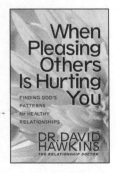

When Pleasing Others Is Hurting You
by David Hawkins

You want to do the right thing—take care of your family, be a good employee, "be there" for your friends. And you're good at it. Everyone knows they can depend on you—so they do.

But are you really doing what's best for them? And what about you? Are you growing? Are you happy and relaxed? Are you excited about your gifts and your calling, or do you sometimes think...*I don't even know what I want anymore.*

In this engaging and provocative book, psychologist David Hawkins will show you why you feel driven to always do more. You'll see how you can actually lose vital parts of your personality and shortchange God's work in your life. And you'll be inspired to rediscover the person God created you to be.